Pearson's Canal Companion

Oxford & Grand Union
& Upper Thames

Published by Wayzgoose
Tatenhill Common
Staffordshire DE13 9RS
email:enquiries@jmpearson.co.uk
www.jmpearson.co.uk

WAYZGOOSE

"WHICH way's Birmingham?" The two well-dressed young Asians on the towpath at Southall looked like they'd strayed from the set of a Bollywood movie. The surprise nature of their simultaneously semaphored enquiry left me momentarily nonplussed. Intuitively, I wanted to point to starboard, or north as it were. But then it occurred to me that they were genuinely intrigued as to which way they would have to follow the canal to reach the second city. Summoning my wits, I gave a big beam and thumbs up to the one who was pointing west, and he rewarded his mistaken companion with an affectionate 'told-you-so' sort of thump on the back.

Steering on, I let go the daydream I'd been enjoying - the fantasy that I was conveying an urgently required consignment of tamarind seeds, loaded at Limehouse for Digbeth - and fell instead to musing on how rare it is to encounter ethnic enthusiasm on the canals. Like train-spotting and fly-fishing, they seem to appeal to a predominantly ageing, Anglo-Saxon demographic. And, heading for Bull's Bridge in splendid solitude - while *Lacewing's* owners lunched below - I sought to analyse the reasons for this apparent indifference by even second and third generation diasporas to the tourist, cultural and historic appeal of the canal system.

It will come as no surprise to serial users of the Canal Companions that the landscapes of my heart lie, almost exclusively, within these shores. Solely that part of northern France previously known as Flanders has ever caught my imagination sufficiently to contemplate what it might be like to jump ship. But here's the thing, when I have been there I have been eager to learn as much of its heritage as possible within the short span of a holiday. Were I to ever live there, I cannot imagine not wanting to embrace as many aspects of its tradition as possible; especially, of course, where its coal mines, breweries, battlefields, railways, football clubs ... and oh yes, its canals are concerned.

Lock-wheeling

So why are immigrants indifferent to the inland waterways? Do we make it hard for them? Does it seem like a closed shop, the arcane world of the canals? You know how over-protective we can be. First-time hire boaters need a tough skin if they are not to be cowed by the know-all demeanor of private boaters. Would it hurt to be a tad more magnanimous? It isn't in anyone's interest that the inland waterways should stultify in a self-defeating clique. In the good old days' of British Waterways there was at least a 'them' to moan about. Now, with all these altruistic, middle-aged, high-vis-vested, buoyancy-aided volunteers about, there only seems to be an incestuous 'us'. But enough wool-gathering. Perhaps you'll bump into my two new Asian chums, loping up the towpath Birmingham-bound on their way to see their Auntie Sunita in Sparkhill. I can only hope they're using a *proper* guide book to get there.

Updating this edition I met a man called Richard and his merry crew at Heyford Common Lock. They appeared to be using several guide books simultaneously. Taking me for a rambler, I was encouraged to mischievously enquire which guide they would recommend? "Oh this one," Richard affirmed to my relief, waving a (regrettably out of date) copy of the Oxford & Grand Union Canal Companion in my direction. "Though the other one's got Ordnance Survey maps which face north ..."

"... which is surely only of significance if you're boating to the North Pole," I witheringly suggested. Much amused, Richard asked: "What's your interest, are you a geographer?"

"No, I'm Pearson's," I confessed. At which Richard leapt acrobatically ashore and pumped me enthusiastically by the hand. Cue for the inevitable lock-side exchange of canaling lingua franca. "We've introduced our friends to your lovely landscape descriptions," enthused Richard's wife, causing me to blush, unbecomingly. Not for the first time it was brought home to me what thoroughly nice folk Canal Companion users invariably are!

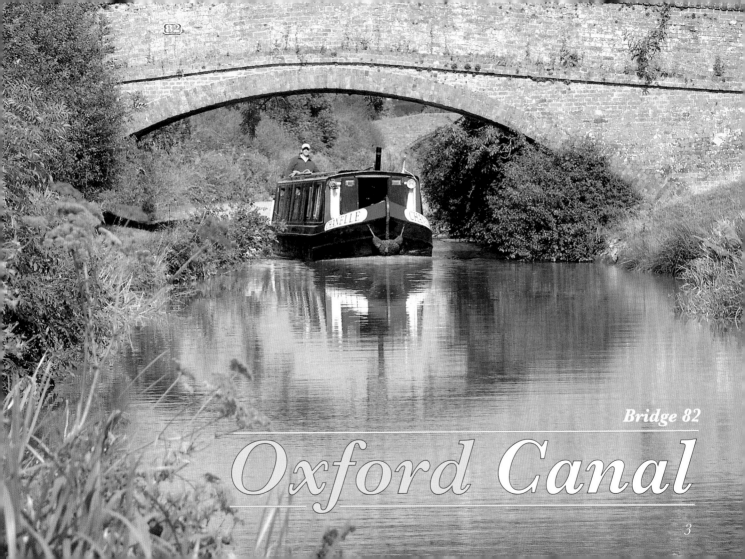

Bridge 82

Oxford Canal

ECCENTRIC though it may seem to begin a guide book devoted to the Oxford Canal where the Coventry and Ashby canals meet at Marston Junction, there is an element of historical rationale, for in working boat days much of the midland coal consigned to the south-east of England originated from mines in the vicinity of Bedworth. And though half a century has passed since the collieries closed and the coal boats departed, the Coventry Canal, skirting the eastern periphery of Bedworth, and encountering housing put up by the Coal Board, remains redolent of all that lost activity in an age which finds it's easier to source coal from Australia than Warwickshire. Indeed, canals have a way of conjuring up the past, and to explore them without being attuned to this important ingredient of their make up would be like listening solely to melody lines at the expense of harmony. Few canal locations demonstrate this more succinctly than Hawkesbury Junction. Hugely popular it may be, with its handsome cast iron bridge, engine house and

Greyhound pub, but to acquire a real feel for Hawkesbury (or 'Sutton Stop' as it was colloquially known) you should obtain a copy of Sonia Rolt's *A Canal People* which features the evocative pictures of local photographer, Robert Longden.

On the acute bend between the Coventry and Oxford canals many a steerer has come to grief in full view of the drinking masses. A stentorian: 'You come and try it mate!' usually silences them, particularly if the embarrassed steerer is of the ostensibly gentler sex. Rumours of a new marina on the site of 'Hawkesbury Light' are rife, but then there are few prime locations these days on the inland waterways where they aren't.

Southwards from Hawkesbury the Oxford Canal commences its lengthy, roundabout journey to the Thames. At Bridge 9 you leave the West Midlands for Warwickshire and a more rural England takes over.

for details of facilities at Hawkesbury turn to page 6

*Figures refer to Oxford Canal only.

THE Oxford Canal slices through the grain of the countryside like someone cutting an appetising slice of fruit pie. But instead of oozing blackberry and apple filling, a rural landscape of shallow valleys and modest rises is exposed. This, however, was not the original course of the canal. Reference to the map will indicate just how tortuous that once was. The embankments and cuttings that characterise the northern section of the Oxford now date from 'shortenings', undertaken between 1829 and 1834, which eliminated no less than fifteen miles between Hawkesbury and Braunston. As surveyed, Brindley's original route stretched the fifteen 'crow' miles between

can clearly be seen amidst less inspirational blocks of flats on the skyline to the south-west. At Nettle Hill the old farm has been converted into a training and conference centre which retains a length of the original canal as a water feature. We came upon eco-friendly towpath repairs in the vicinity of Coombe fields on our most recent research trip, but this is still not a length of canal to cycle beside.

Canal and railway share an embankment near Brinklow, scene of many well known photographs and paintings depicting narrowboats and steam trains in quaint juxtaposition; the tortoises and hares, respectively, of 19th century transport. These days the disparity in velocity is even greater; those Pendolinos are going *forty* times faster than you.

Stretton Stop was formerly a point at which tolls were taken. The scene here today is invariably busy and colourful. The old arm to Stretton Wharf is used for private moorings and as access to a boatyard. Some of the original buildings remain at the wharf which once featured a series of lime kilns.

for details of facilities at Ansty and Brinklow turn to page 6

Coventry and Napton into a staggering forty-three miles of convoluted canal. Brindley didn't care. He felt that the more places his canal visited, the more influence and commerce one might accrue. No-one expected canal transport to be fast. Its benefits lay in convenience and reliability. Even after the improvements old sections remained in use serving businesses and wharves already established on their banks.

Like an erring tee-shot, the canal *slices* across Ansty Golf Centre, an eighteen hole municipal course. From the elevated position of the 'new' embankment, the remaining spires of the original Coventry cathedral

Back on the mainline, boaters should take care not to collide with the foot swing-bridge which links the towpath side with the boat-building sheds of Rose Narrowboats on the opposite bank. Three significant roads cross the canal. The M6 and M69 motorways will have to wait a bit longer to gain affection in most people's hearts, but the Fosse Way - the Roman Road which once linked Lincoln with Exeter - encounters the canal on the outskirts of Brinklow.

Train racing, Brinklow

Hawkesbury
Map 1

THE GREYHOUND - canalside. Tel: 02476 363046. Famous waterside pub which has catered for generations of boaters. Regular recipient of local CAMRA awards. CV6 6DF

Ansty
Map 2

Surrounded by motorways, Ansty lacks obvious interest, though the sequestered Victorian church boasts a mock medieval steeple. Once upon a time the villlage was a centre for ribbon-making.

Eating & Drinking

ROSE & CASTLE - Main Road. Tel: 02476 612822. Vaguely canal-themed roadside pub with large garden spilling down to the canal. Access via bridges 14 or 16. CV7 9HZ

Connections

BUSES - services 74/5 operate bi-hourly to/from Coventry. Tel: 0871 200 2233.

Brinklow
Map 2

Brinklow's agreeably wide main street is framed by an enjoyable miscellany of building styles and periods. A house called Tallow Cottage recalls the existence of a candle factory. At the northern edge of the village a pair of timber gates denote the location of a former wharf which lay on the old route of the canal. Past the Perpendicular church a footpath leads up to the motte & bailey outline of a Norman castle known affectionately by locals as 'The Tump', and worth scaling for an extensive panorama of rural Warwickshire. Yes, Brinklow is one of the best villages to visit along the 'northern' section of the Oxford Canal, but do *beware* of the Fosse Way traffic which moves much faster than the Romans ever envisaged and takes far fewer prisoners in the process.

Eating & Drinking

THE RAVEN - Broad Street. Tel: 01788 832655. Marston's local. CV23 0LN

WHITE LION - Broad Street. Tel: 01788 832579. Former half-timbered coaching inn fronting on to village street, serving Banks's beer and offering food and accommodation. CV23 0LN

PUMPKINS DELI - Broad Street. Tel: 01788 833094. Charming coffee shop offering paninis, bloomers, omelettes, soups, quiches, ploughmans etc. CV23 0LS *The village also boasts a third pub (Bull's Head - Tel: 01788 832355), fish & chip shop (Tel: 01788 832766) and Chinese takeaway (Tel: 01788 833257).*

Shopping

The boatyard shop stocks provisions, but in the village, about ten minutes pavemented walk from the canal, you'll additionally find a post office stores. Pumpkins delicatessen (see E & D) provides a wide range of quality provisions.

Connections

BUSES - service 585 operates half-hourly daily to/from Coventry and Rugby. Tel: 0871 200 2233.

3 OXFORD CANAL

PROBABLY at its prettiest, the 'Northern Oxford' moves languidly from bridge-hole to bridge-hole in no apparent rush to get to Coventry or Rugby, or anywhere else for that matter. And herein lies perhaps the greatest secret of canal travel: by removing the 'aims' and 'targets' with which we are apt to litter our highly stressed lives, a calmer, stress-free existence emerges, enabling all us inland waterway Houdinis to escape our self-imposed chains and bounds more effectively than those slaves to sun tans on exotic beaches.

'Brinklow Arches', originally a twelve-arched aqueduct carrying the canal over Smite Brook, was replaced by an embankment during the mid-nineteenth century improvements. Bridge 32 carries the 'modernised' towpath over the original route, retained as an arm to serve Brinklow. The depth of the 'new' cutting is considerable. It was the work of fledgling engineers Cubitt and Vignoles, both of whom were to make their reputations during the railway era. Several wet winters seem to have re-watered the arm. The former Fellows Morton & Clayton steamer *Earl* had its back broken in 1930 and was ignominiously towed to a marshy grave on the edge of Brinklow where its skeleton remains, albeit officially out of bounds. The redbrick, Italianate pile known as Town Thorns was

designed by Alfred Waterhouse for an American magistrate called Washington Jackson. During the Second World War the house provided sanctuary for children evacuated from Coventry. Now it is a care home.

At intervals, other sections of the original route join and leave the canal beneath the spans of elegant cast-iron bridges made by the Horseley Iron Works Company of Tipton whose structures proliferate on the BCN. These reedy old arms are, for the most part, no longer remotely navigable; which is a shame, for they would have made delightful mooring backwaters. However, fresh use of the Fennis Field Arm has recently been made to access Brinklow Marina. The towpaths of the old arms have vanished as well, rendering them unexplorable even on foot, though here and there an ancient bridge remains stranded surreally and mysteriously in the midst of some field or other.

At Newbold the original course of the canal was considerably shortened by the construction of a new tunnel in 1829. Recently it has been provided with a light display, switched off at sunset so as not to disturb the bats! Those with an enthusiasm for such things can discover one of the bricked up portals of the original tunnel at the north-western edge of St Botolph's churchyard. This change of route explains why the "Boat Inn" seems to have nothing to do with the canal it once fronted on to. The Newbold Arm was kept in water to supply water troughs on the neighbouring railway.

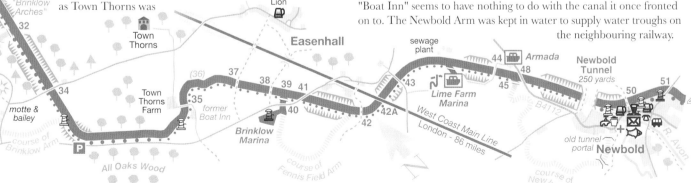

for details of facilities at Easenhall and Newbold turn to page 9

7

4 OXFORD CANAL Rugby & Hillmorton 4mls/3lks/2hrs

THE saving in distance achieved by the 19th century improvements to the Oxford Canal is nowhere more apparent than in the vicinity of Rugby. In order to keep to the 300ft contour and minimise earthworks, the original route went wandering off a couple of miles to the north, looking for a convenient point to cross the River Swift. Then, having returned to the outskirts of Rugby via Brownsover, it set off again, this time to cross the River Avon near Clifton-on-Dunsmore.

The outskirts of Rugby are not especially pretty, but neither are they dull. Retail parks, ring roads, industrial units, housing estates and all the other accumulated junk of modern day life are paraded for the canal traveller's contempt. Cubitt's new route involved a sequence of aqueducts and embankments across the wide valleys of the Swift and Avon which form a confluence just to the south. It makes for a fascinating journey to this day, conifers masking the proximity of factories and shops, and there is barely a dull

moment as the entrances and exits of the old loops are passed, and you try to do a Sherlock Holmes (or should that now be a Sarah Lund?) on the topography of the original canal. A footpath leads enticingly along the old Brownsover Arm which can be followed all the way to the remains of Cosford Aqueduct where it spanned the Swift. There are lost railways to decipher as well. The Midland, London & North Western and Great Central all converged on Rugby, all crossed the canal, and were all abandoned in the nineteen-sixties.

By road, Rugby and Hillmorton are inseparable. The canal, though, takes its time in travelling between the two, dallying in the fields before a widening, fringed by reed beds, heralds the first of three duplicated locks carrying the canal up past the Oxford Canal Company's dignified workshops, framed by Bridge 70. Lock No.2 features rare iron gates, refurbished in 2011.

Hillmorton's canalscape has a backdrop of wireless masts - a dozen of the tallest being 820ft high - of necessity lit red at night to ward off low-flying aircraft. Rugby Radio Station dates from 1926 and was used to operate the first trans-Atlantic radio telephone link between London and New York. Nowadays the station transmits telecommunications all over the world, though after eighty years it lost the contract to broadcast time signals on behalf of the Royal Observatory.

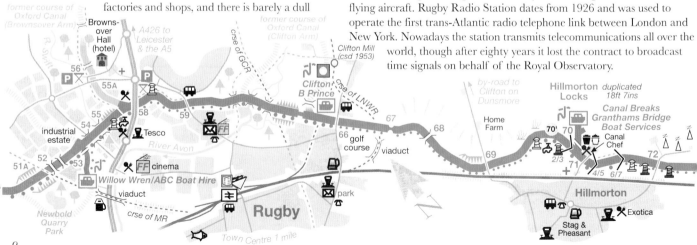

Easenhall

Map 3

Picturesque village reached by footpaths over or under the railway.

Eating & Drinking

GOLDEN LION - village centre. Tel: 01788 833577. *Good Pub Guide* listed country inn and restaurant open for lunch (from noon) daily and dinner (from 5.30pm. Sunday carvery. Accommodation. CV23 0JA

Newbold on Avon

Map 3

With its church, canal wharf, and access to the infant River Avon, Newbold is a pleasant enough suburb of Rugby - useful for the replenishment of stores.

Eating & Drinking

BARLEY MOW - Tel: 01788 544174. Bar/restaurant food, pool, darts & skittles, patio and beer garden. Bath and laundry facilities available for boaters. Has absorbed the neighbouring Boat Inn for functions. CV21 1HW

There is also a fish & chip shop in Newbold and another pub down in the village.

Shopping

Co-op store/post office with cash machine.

Connections

BUSES - services 3/3A and 585 run frequently to/from Rugby. Tel: 0871 200 2233.

Rugby

Map 4

Rugby's reputation is inextricably linked with its famous public school. Founded in 1567, it wasn't until its best known headmaster, Dr Arnold, arrived on the scene in 1828 that the glory years ensued. Ever since, Rugby has held its place among the top schools in the country, and a steady stream of former pupils have gone on to make their mark on the world. Ironically, it was a boy casually flouting 'unwritten' rules who made the greatest gesture of all when, one day in 1823, to alleviate the boredom of a football match, he picked up the ball and ran with it, thereby founding the game of 'rugby'. A statue on the corner of Lawrence Sheriff Street and Dunchurch Road commemorates William Webb Ellis's defiant gesture, depicting him in full flight. There are also statues in the town of Thomas Hughes, former pupil and author of *Tom Brown's Schooldays*, and Rupert Brooke, son of a Rugby housemaster. Rugby School's past roll-call is particularly rich in such literary figures, and includes Matthew Arnold (son of the headmaster), 'Lewis Carroll', and Walter Savage Landor.

Eating & Drinking

BELL & BARGE - canalside Bridge 58. Tel: 01788 569466. Harvester restaurant. CV21 1HL
BUTLER'S LEAP - Clifton Road (SW Bridge 66). Tel: 01788 577650. Whitbread 'Table Table' restaurant open from noon daily. CV21 3TX
CAFE VIN CINQ - High Street. Tel: 01788 541304. French cafe/bistro opposite Rugby School. CV21 3BW
CANAL CHEF - canalside at Hillmorton. Tel: 01788 567600. Charming canal-centric cafe and beer garden fronted by motor *Badsey* and butty *Angel*. Open daily Mar-Oct, 9am-6pm plus Friday evenings. CV21 4PP
EXOTICA - Lower Street, Hillmorton. Tel: 01788 547187. Bengal cuisine, open evenings daily from 5.30pm (5pm Fri & Sat). CV21 4NU
FERGUSON'S - Eastfield Place. Tel: 01788 550222. Warehouse conversion brasserie formerly known as Vermillion. Open Tue-Sat from 6pm and Sat & Sun lunchtimes. CV21 3AT
MERCHANTS INN - Little Church Street. Tel: 01788 571119. CAMRA'S *Good Beer Guide* holds this town centre pub in high esteem for its breweriana, comfort and wide choice of real ales. CV21 3AW
THE OLD ROYAL OAK - Bridge 73 (Map 9). Tel: 01788 561401. A Greene King 'Hungry Horse' pub. Pleasant garden and moorings. CV21 4PW
RUGBY TAP - St Matthews St. Tel: 01788 576767. Micropub and bottled beer shop. CV21 3BY

STAG & PHEASANT - School Street, Hillmorton. Tel: 01788 331228. Suburban pub serving food Thur-Sat evening and Sun lunch. CV21 4BW
SUMMERSAULT - High Street. Tel: 01788 543223. Delightful wholefood cafe and restaurant housed in handsome terracotta building formerly belonging to Boots the Chemist. Jazz on Friday evenings. Also deals in imaginative gifts. CV21 3BW

Shopping

A large Tesco stands conveniently adjacent to the canal at Bridge 58, otherwise all facilities are to be found in the town centre just over a mile south of Bridge 59 from whence bus service 4 operates at frequent intervals. Rugby is a comprehensive shopping centre without being overpowering, and in addition to the standard chain stores there are a fair number of long established local retailers. Outdoor markets are held on Mondays, Fridays and Saturdays. Farmers Market last Thursday of each month.

Things to Do

TOURIST INFORMATION - Rugby Art Gallery and Museum. Tel: 01788 533217. CV21 3BZ
RUGBY ART GALLERY & MUSEUM - Little Elborow Street. Tel: 01788 533201. Rugby's showpiece cultural attraction. Modern art, the Tripontium Collection of Roman artefacts, and social history objects relating to the town. Open daily ex Mon. CV21 3BZ
RUGBY FOOTBALL MUSEUM - St Matthews Street. Tel: 01788 533217. Place of pilgrimage for lovers of the oval ball game. Open Mon-Sat, 9am-5pm, admission free. CV21 3BY
RUGBY SCHOOL MUSEUM - Barby Road. Tel: 01788 556169. Museum open Mon-Sat. Guided tours Mon, Fri & Sat. CV21 3AW

Connections

BUSES - throughout the area - Tel: 0871 200 2233.
TRAINS - Virgin/London Midland services from station half a mile south of Bridge 59. Tel: 08457 484950.
TAXIS - People Express. Tel: 01788 565888.

5 OXFORD CANAL Willoughby 5mls/0lks/2hrs

BETWEEN Rugby and Braunston the Oxford Canal plays hopscotch with Warwickshire and Northamptonshire as the border twists back and forth like all good county boundaries, drawn up in the mists of antiquity, should. This is the old Feldon region - the land south of Avon - exemplified by a rolling, sparsely wooded countryside; plain to the eye of the casual beholder, but full of interest if you are prepared to delve deeper. Remnants of medieval 'ridge & furrow' farming remain evident in pastures bordering the canal. These patterns, zig-zagging across the fields, were preserved because this former arable land - where each ridge represented the individual strip of a peasant farmer - was given over to pasture immediately after the area was enclosed by hawthorn hedges at some time between the 15th and 17th centuries. This also explains the dearth of settlements in the area, whole communities being torn down and peasants sent packing by ruthless landowners, to make way for the new, more profitable field system.

The canal's past is ever present too. More of its old meanderings can be detected. At the north-east end of the shallow cutting by Bridge 77, look into the field on the towpath side and you'll see the original bed of the canal, an obvious declivity parallel with the neighbouring hedgerow.

Dating from 1959, the M45 is comparatively underused now, a quaint white elephant of the early Motorway Age. Why, there is even an unwitting charm in its concrete structures. An even older use of that much maligned material can be found between bridges 78 and 79 where the towpath is bounded by Oxford Canal Company concrete fence posts bearing the company's initials.

Opened in 1897, the Great Central Railway was the last main line to be built in Britain, its promoters having visions of linking the north of England with mainland Europe by way of a tunnel under the Channel. A hundred years too early in its aspirations, it was myopically abandoned in 1966. Near Bridge 85 the concrete post of Braunston & Willoughby's 'Up Distant' signal waits faithfully for the Marylebone-bound 'Master Cutler' to puff proudly by behind *Galtee More*, *Solario* or *Sir Frederick Banbury*.

Though designated the "Oxford Canal Walk" the 'North' Oxford's towpath between Hillmorton and Braunston remains unsurfaced and in places erosion has reduced its width. At least, on our most recent research trip, the vegetation had been cleared and the surface grass mown - though not always to the water's edge! Cycling cannot be recommended with a clear conscience.

Saisons Hillmorton Wharf
Canal Shop
former wharf & stables
Barby Moorings
Warwickshire
Whitehall Farm
OCC posts
Onley Fields Farm
HM Prison
fishery
Barby Wood Farm
Onley Marina (under const.)
Northamptonshire
ridge & furrow
crse of Great Central Railway
former course of Oxford Canal
Willoughby Wharf
old signal
ridge & furrow
by-road Willough
Warwickshire
B4038 to Kilsby
NORTHAMPTON LONDON
A428
former course of Oxford Canal

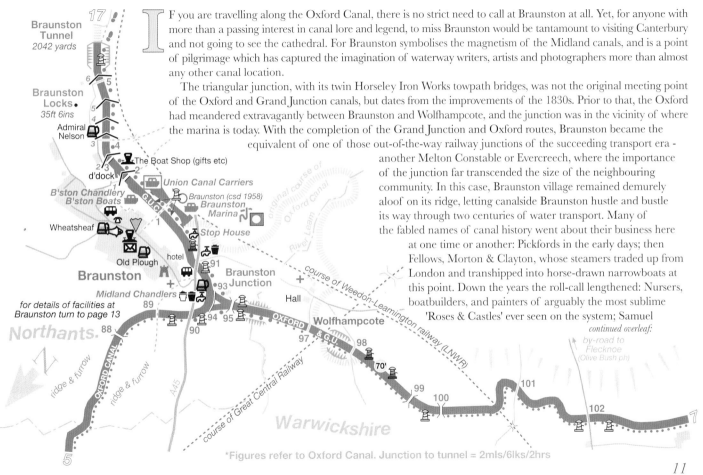

Braunston Tunnel 2042 yards

Braunston Locks 35ft 6ins

Admiral Nelson

The Boat Shop (gifts etc)

d'dock

B'ston Chandlery B'ston Boats

Wheatsheaf

Old Plough

hotel

Braunston

Midland Chandlers

for details of facilities at Braunston turn to page 13

Northants.

ridge & furrow

ridge & furrow

OXFORD CANAL

Union Canal Carriers

Braunston (csd 1958)

Braunston Marina

Stop House

original course of Oxford Canal

River Leam

course of Weedon-Leamington railway (LNWR)

Braunston Junction

Hall

Wolfhampcote

OXFORD & G.U.

course of Great Central Railway

Warwickshire

by-road to Flecknoe (Olive Bush ph)

IF you are travelling along the Oxford Canal, there is no strict need to call at Braunston at all. Yet, for anyone with more than a passing interest in canal lore and legend, to miss Braunston would be tantamount to visiting Canterbury and not going to see the cathedral. For Braunston symbolises the magnetism of the Midland canals, and is a point of pilgrimage which has captured the imagination of waterway writers, artists and photographers more than almost any other canal location.

The triangular junction, with its twin Horseley Iron Works towpath bridges, was not the original meeting point of the Oxford and Grand Junction canals, but dates from the improvements of the 1830s. Prior to that, the Oxford had meandered extravagantly between Braunston and Wolfhampcote, and the junction was in the vicinity of where the marina is today. With the completion of the Grand Junction and Oxford routes, Braunston became the equivalent of one of those out-of-the-way railway junctions of the succeeding transport era - another Melton Constable or Evercreech, where the importance of the junction far transcended the size of the neighbouring community. In this case, Braunston village remained demurely aloof on its ridge, letting canalside Braunston hustle and bustle its way through two centuries of water transport. Many of the fabled names of canal history went about their business here at one time or another: Pickfords in the early days; then Fellows, Morton & Clayton, whose steamers traded up from London and transhipped into horse-drawn narrowboats at this point. Down the years the roll-call lengthened: Nursers, boatbuilders, and painters of arguably the most sublime 'Roses & Castles' ever seen on the system; Samuel

continued overleaf:

Figures refer to Oxford Canal. Junction to tunnel = 2mls/6lks/2hrs

continued from page 11:

Barlow, the coal carriers whose boats were always in the most pristine of condition; and, towards the end, Willow Wren and Blue Line, who kept canal carrying defiantly afloat into the era of the juggernaut.

But the working boats have gone, and with them, inevitably, something of Braunston's old magic. Nevertheless, this is still a flourishing canal centre, home to a hire fleet and a large marina based on former reservoirs, as well as numerous canal-based industries from boatbuilders to suppliers of traditional boater's wear. Wander along the towpath and you'll see new boats being built, old ones restored, and a regular stream of traffic up and down the locks, and it only takes the aroma of a charcoal stove, the beat of a Bolinder, or the rattle of the ratchets in the twilight of an autumn afternoon for the old days to be almost tangibly evoked.

Six wide beam locks carry the Grand Union up to the mouth of Braunston Tunnel. Water and energy can be saved by working through them in company. Passage in under an hour is eminently possible given sufficient enthusiasm. Braunston Tunnel takes about twenty minutes to negotiate. What happens at the other end is detailed on Map 17.

The five mile section between Braunston and Napton is interesting scenically and historically. It is a thoroughly remote length of canal; the countryside falling flatly away to the north-west, but climbing abruptly to a notable ridge in the opposite direction. There are ghosts and echoes everywhere: reedy old loops; abandoned railways; lost villages; and, at Wolfhampcote, the splendidly isolated medieval church of St Peter where services are extremely rare, but which hosts an annual carol concert on the second Saturday in December. Cared for now by the estimable Churches Conservation Trust, access to the atmospheric interior can be facilitated by collecting the key from an adjacent cottage.

When the Grand Union Canal was formed in 1929, there remained a gap between its former Grand Junction (London-Braunston) and Warwick & Napton constituents which belonged to the Oxford Canal. Knowing a good thing when they saw it, the Oxford company kindly allowed the Grand Union to pick up the tab for a programme of dredging and concrete banking, at the same time continuing to extract tolls from them until Nationalisation.

A phenomenon relating to this 'joint' length is that boats travelling between the Midlands and the South, via either the Oxford or the Grand Union, pass each other going in the opposite direction; shades of the Great Western and Southern railways at Exeter, or the GWR and LMS at Chester. Should you have an interest in railways, you might do worse than leave the canal for a moment or two and go exploring the old trackbeds and earthworks of the former Great Central and London & North Western lines which crossed each other at Wolfhampcote. A handsome blue brick occupation bridge, typical of the GCR's London Extension, spans a broad cutting to the south.

Bridge 1, Braunston

Braunston Marina

Bottom Lock

Braunston

Map 6

Village Braunston demurely straddles its ridge, four hundred feet up on the slopes of the Northamptonshire uplands. Enclosed fields, still bearing the pattern of ridge & furrow, distil the spirit of the Middle Ages. Sauntering along the High Street from the village green to the tall crockett-spired church (nicknamed the Cathedral of the Canals and last resting place of a number of working boat men and women) one encounters a mixture of stone and brick buildings, including a sail-less windmill (available for holiday lets - Tel: 01788 220178) and a 17th century manor house. At the foot of a long hill the A45 crosses the canal. This was the Chester turnpike road which predates the canal and which was once used by Leslie Morton as an office. Restaurant and bar meals, attractive garden. Northamptonshire skittles. NN11 7HJ

Braunston Church

Eating & Drinking
ADMIRAL NELSON - canalside Bridge 4. Tel: 01788 890075. Refurbished canalside inn, which predates the canal and which was once used by Leslie Morton as an office. Restaurant and bar meals, attractive garden. Northamptonshire skittles. NN11 7HJ

THE BOAT HOUSE - canalside Bridge 91. Tel: 01788 891734. Marston's 'Two for One' family pub with customer moorings. NN11 7HB

BRAUNSTON FRYER - The Green. Tel: 01788 890258. Fish & chips/kebabs/pizzas etc open Tue-Fri from 3pm and Sat from noon. NN11 7HW

GONGOOZLER'S REST - cafe aboard a boat moored alongside the Stop House.

OLD OLIVE BUSH - Flecknoe. Tel: 01788 891134. Charming village pub idyllically approachable on foot from Braunston via Wolfhampcote or by mooring in the vicinity of bridges 101 or 102 and walking up to Flecknoe, a mile from the canal. CV23 8AT

OLD PLOUGH - High Street. Tel: 01788 878126. One of two village 'locals'. Food, lunch and evening daily (ex Sunday evening). NN11 7HS

WHEATSHEAF - village centre. Tel: 01788 890748. Chinese food (890503) to eat in or carry out, Saturday evening rock gigs. NN11 7HW

YOUR CAFE - High Street. Community cafe. Gifts, teas, ice creams and homemade cakes. NN11 7HR

Shopping
Facilities include a post office and convenience store - open from 6am to 7.30pm (6pm Sun) - who advertise that they are happy to deliver to your boat (Tel: 01788 890334), and an enterprising butcher who additionally deals in hot pies and filled rolls. Down by the canal, alongside the bottom lock, The Boat Shop (Tel: 01788 891310) opens from 8am-8pm throughout the summer season and deals in just about everything from gifts to groceries and friendly local knowledge.

Connections
BUSES - Stagecoach service 12 operates hourly Mon-Sat to/from Rugby and Daventry. Tel: 0871 200 2233.

7 OXFORD CANAL Napton & Marston Doles 6mls/9lks/4hrs

AT Napton Junction (known to working boatmen as Wigrams Turn) the Oxford Canal sets off southwards on its long, winding road to the River Thames. Despite the proximity of two busy marinas, the junction itself is typically remote. A 1930s concrete bridge spans the entrance and exit of the Grand Union route, formerly the Warwick & Napton Canal. Interestingly, it is numbered 17. Where (we can hear you wondering) are the other sixteen? The answer is that they were in the Grand Union Company's imagination. When they acquired rights to the route from Braunston to Birmingham in 1929 they re-numbered the sequence of bridges from Braunston northwards, including those on the Oxford Canal as far as Napton which never actually bore the GU numbers allocated to them.

East of Napton the shared section of the Oxford and Grand Union routes pursues its lonely course, passing the small settlement of Lower Shuckburgh and its picturesque Victorian church. A footpath climbs from here through parkland to the medieval village of Upper Shuckburgh. The name is said to mean 'a hill haunted by goblins'. Certainly Beacon Hill, rising to 678 feet, has its spirits. A 17th century member of the Shuckburgh family is said to have been accosted by King Charles I whilst hunting on the hill. The King, on his way to fight at the Battle of Edgehill, demanded to know how an English gentleman could spare time for hunting when his King was fighting for his crown.

Whilst the Grand Union heads determinedly off towards Birmingham, the more poetically-minded Oxford picks its way quietly around the hem of Napton Hill, a gentle summit half-eaten away by old quarry workings. For the best part of a

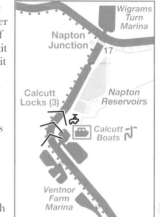

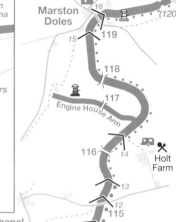

Though designated the 'Oxford Canal Walk', between Braunston and Banbury the quality of the towpath fluctuates from passable to poor, particularly if it's been a while since the mowing contractors' last visit.

14

century, clay was extracted from the hill and used in the manufacture of bricks at the works by Bridge 112. Narrowboats carried the finished products to Napton railway station on the Warwick & Napton Canal, a couple of miles north of Napton Junction.

Napton Locks lift the canal up to the hamlet of Marston Doles. Mostly you seem to breeze through, but queues can occur at the height of summer. You used to be able to measure your progress by reference to the windmill, but as the years go by it appears to be disappearing below the tree line. Water buffalo graze incongruously in fields beside the canal. Indigenous to south-east Asia, they have been successfully farmed in Napton for a number of years.

In the lengthy pound between the top two locks and the rest, a branch canal leaves the main line and appears to head off across the fields towards Beacon Hill. This is the Engine House Arm, dug to enable boats to bring coal to a stationary steam engine which once pumped water through a system of channels and pipes back to the summit section; the arm is now in use as a backwater for linear moorings. The top lock is overlooked by a handsome, trapezium-shaped warehouse, nowadays in use as offices. Thence the summit stretches beguilingly ahead. The next lock being five hours boating away. Hip, hip, hooray!

Napton on the Hill   Map 7

Napton (best reached from Bridge 113) basks in the sunshine (or shivers when a gale blows) on its south-facing hill. Ochre stone and thatch characterise the older buildings, brick the infills. Its street pattern takes some fathoming, but there is much green space between the houses and even the seemingly obligatory modern developments dovetail neatly into the whole. Sheltered in the lee from north-easterlies, the parish church of St Lawrence has a Norman chancel with a sundial. You can climb towards the windmill for a better view, but it is on private property and never open to the public.

Eating & Drinking

THE BRIDGE - canalside Bridge 111. Tel: 01926 257575. Bar & restaurant meals and pleasant garden with adjacent moorings. Closed Tue. CV47 8NQ
THE FOLLY - adjacent Bridge 113. Tel: 01926 815185. Quaint pub at foot of locks long ago known as "The Bull & Butcher". CV47 8NZ
KING'S HEAD - on A425 south of Bridge 109. Tel: 01926 812202. Comfortably refurbished Hook Norton inn with a good choice of food. CV47 8NG
NAPTON KITCHEN - cafe/take-away in village shop.

Fenny 'Tunnel'

Shopping

Napton lies half a mile east of Bridge 113 and boasts a vibrant post office stores (Tel: 01926 812488 - CV47 8LR) open 7am-7pm Mon-Sat and 8am-2pm Sun. They are particularly proud of their locally sourced produce which ranges from honey and preserves to water buffalo burgers, sausages, steaks, cheese and ice cream.

Connections

BUSES - service 65 runs to/from Daventry, Southam and Leamington bi-hourly Mon-Sat. Tel: 0871 200 2233.

Fenny Compton   Map 8

Remote Warwickshire village which has its own water supply from a spring in the nearby hills.

Eating & Drinking

THE WHARF - canalside Bridge 136. Tel: 01295 770332. Canalside inn offering a good choice of food in comfortable surroundings. Large canalside garden. Shop offering provisions and bottled gas, launderette, campsite, and even a unisex hair salon.
MERRIE LION - Brook Street (village centre, 1 mile west of canal). Tel: 01295 771134. Comfortably refurbished pub re-opened with financial investment from local shareholders. Real ales and food. CV47 2XF

Shopping

See The Wharf above, but also Co-op store (with cash machine) in village and out-reach post office in village hall Mon, Wed & Fri am.

Connections

BUSES - service 277 runs twice-daily to Banbury via Cropredy. Tel: 0871 200 2233.

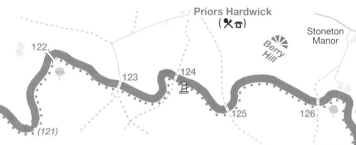

Wormleighton sleeps the sleep of the innocent on a gentle slope overlooking the canal's meanderings. Chief delight is the gatehouse dating from 1613, built from local stone the colour of a weather-beaten face. South of the wharf at Fenny Compton the canal negotiates a deep, narrow cutting. When the canal was first built there was a thousand yard tunnel here. But the rock was brittle and the bore a bottleneck, and in time the top was taken off. Bridge 137A is an elegant cast iron turnover bridge carrying the towpath from one side to the other. It is dwarfed by a modern concrete structure carrying the A423. By Bridge 138 a kiln used to make bricks during construction of the canal has been earmarked for restoration.

Priors Hardwick

BUTCHERS ARMS - Church End. Tel: 01327 260504. Fine dining in 14thC inn reached on foot from bridges 123-5. CV47 7SN

FOR eleven dizzy, dreamy miles the Oxford Canal traverses its depopulated summit. With a compass, a pair of stout walking shoes and a healthy disregard for the laws of trespass, you could do it in four. But because - as the poet Edward Thomas put it - 'there is nothing at the end of any road better than can be found beside it' - you feel no desire to count the miles, no temptation to begrudge Brindley his watershed wanderings.

We used to say that the Oxford's summit was as shallow as a matinee idol's smile, but dredging in recent years has increased the depth of water available and it is now perfectly feasible to average something in the region of three miles an hour. If only the towpath was equally well-maintained. A crisp winter's day is probably the best time to walk the summit. Summer's brambles have a tendency to wrap themselves around your neck. Bike it? Only masochists need apply.

The loneliness of the summit has always evoked a mystic, trance-inducing quality. That may be about to change if HS2 ever gets off the drawing board. For the new high speed railway line from London to Birmingham is earmarked to cross the canal between bridges 127 and 128.

for details of facilities at Fenny Compton turn back to page 15

9 OXFORD CANAL Claydon & Cropredy 5mls/9lks/3hrs

THE Oxford Canal commences its drawn out descent to the Thames. Northwards, Claydon marks the start of the summit section; no more locks to work for four or five hours! Wormleighton, Boddington and Clattercote are not, as you might erroneously assume, a litigious firm of Banbury solicitors, but rather the three reservoirs which feed the Oxford Canal. Water shortages have always been a problem on this waterway and at times the density of pleasure traffic exacerbates the situation.

Bridge 141 straddles the county boundary and is the northernmost of the characteristic draw bridges synonymous with this canal. They are simplicity defined, consisting of no more than a pair of shallow brick abutments, a platform and two hefty timber balance beams set at 45 degrees when the bridge is closed to boats, or flat against the nettles when, as is often the case, they are left open. Seen from afar, they punctuate the

Oxford Canal's passage through the Cherwell Valley, as homogeneous with this landscape as the pollarded willows of its watermeadows and the oolite stonework of its villages.

The course of the old Stratford & Midland Junction Railway parallels the canal by Bridge 142 which spans the feeder from Boddington Reservoir. The railway was one of those forgotten little lines whose high hopes were never realised. It became disparagingly, but affectionately known as the 'Slow, Mouldy and Jolting'. L. T. C. Rolt loved the unhurried progress of its trains, their "slow, panting climbs, and swift, swaying descents" across the Northamptonshire uplands.

At Claydon Top Lock, the Oxford Canal Company's workshops remain evident. This would have been a busy spot in the heyday of the canal. Three isolated locks interrupt the canal's otherwise uneventful progress between Claydon and Cropredy where a large new marina opened in 2013. In the centre of the village the canal narrows by the old toll office and manager's house, whilst south of Bridge 153 a former coal wharf provides boating facilities and room to turn a seventy footer.

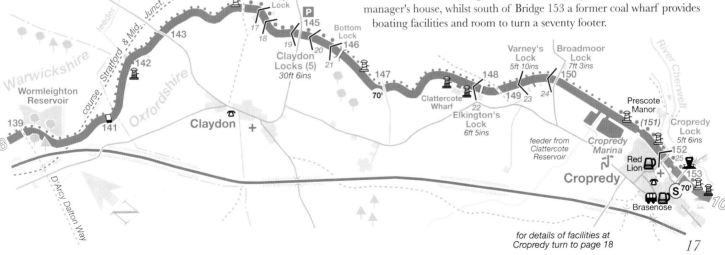

for details of facilities at Cropredy turn to page 18

17

Cropredy
Map 9

Cropredy is the village with the closest relationship to the Oxford Canal and, as such, makes an ideal place to break your journey, whether on foot or afloat. It has become famous in folk music circles as the location of an annual (August) festival centred round the enduring folk rock group *Fairport Convention*. But this is one music festival where locals and visitors seem in harmony: the Brasenose Arms even featured on the back cover of Fairport's 9th album.

You have to go back over three hundred years to the other most significant event in Cropredy's mellow existence. There was a Civil War battle here in 1644. Ten thousand men took part and some of the clobber they left behind - helmets, bayonets and cannon balls - used to be on display in the church: until it was recently stolen, that is. One survival, however, is an eagle-headed lectern made of brass which was apparently submerged in the Cherwell to keep it safe from the marauding Puritans. Ralph McTell's song *Red & Gold* illuminates this period in Cropredy's history. Cropredy Cricket Club's (founded 1927) picturesque ground lies a short walk east of Bridge 153.

Eating & Drinking
THE RED LION - 100 yards west of Bridge 152. Tel: 01295 758680. Thatched village inn visited by Temple Thurston (*The Flower of Gloster*) and L.T.C. Rolt (*Narrow Boat*). It has lost little of its charm: sunbeams still slant through the neighbouring churchyard and glint on your pint. Post office 'outreach' facility on Mon & Wed mornings. OX17 1PB

THE BRASENOSE ARMS - 300 yards west of Bridge 153. Tel: 01295 750244. Nicely furnished country pub offering food lunchtimes and evenings daily, bed & breakfast and laundry facilities. Live bands on Saturday evenings. OX17 1PW

Shopping
BRIDGE STORES by Bridge 153 is open daily stocking groceries, wines & spirits, newspapers, cash machine and Calor gas. Nostalgic collection of Fairport's Cropredy Convention posters on display.

Connections
BUSES - service 277 provides a sparse link with Banbury and Fenny 'C', Mon-Sat. Tel: 0871 200 2233.

Banbury
Map 10

Aromatic home to Mondelez - manufacturers of Kenco, Cafe Noire, and Tassimo coffee capsules - together with six thousand Poles (and counting!), this upwardly mobile market town provides boaters with useful shopping, cultural and commercial facilities, and yet its soul remains elusive. In a town of handsome, though not necessarily appreciated buildings, one of our favourites is Lampreys, a former corn merchants by the market place, its upper storey a signwritten reminder of Banbury's importance as an agricultural centre: up until 1998 the town was the location of a massive cattle market. The late eighteenth century church is worth seeking out if you've an enthusiasm for classical architecture. The town has not forgotten its niche in the pantheon of nursery rhymes, and a replica cross (erected by the Victorians following removal of the original by a Puritan mob in 1600) can still be seen at the southern end of The Horsefair.

Eating & Drinking
CAFE RED - canalside Bridge 164. Tel: 01295 270444. Light and airy eating place. Coffees, teas, lunches plus summer evening meals with a Greek twist. OX16 2PA

THAI ORCHID - North Bar. Tel: 01295 262969. Flamboyant ethnic restaurant and take-away up at the far end of the town. OX16 0TL

PIZZA CALZONE - Parson's Street. Tel: 01295 703073. Italian restaurant and take-away. OX16 5NA

YE OLDE REINDEER INN - Parsons Street (west of market place). Tel: 01295 264031. *Good Beer Guide* listed inn dating from 1570. Hook Norton ales. OX16 5NA

COACH & HORSES - Butchers Row. Tel: 01295 256550. Contemporary town centre pub offering lunch and dinner Mon-Sat and Sun lunch. OX16 5JH

LITTLE AMSTERDAM - North Bar. Tel: 01295 279140. Pancake house open Tue-Sun from 10am. OX16 0TF

Shopping
The canalside Castle Quay shopping centre likes to think that it has put upstart Milton Keynes in its place, but, better still, is the lively Farmer's Market held on the first Friday of each month. Certainly as far as canal travellers are concerned there's no excuse for not laying in stores. One or two Polish shops reflect new blood in the community. There's a good bookshop (Books & Ink: new & s/h) tucked away at the top of White Lion Walk. Tesco is a tad tricky for boaters to access. We suggest walking from Bridge 163 via Marley Way and the coffee works; about 10 minutes.

Things to Do
MUSEUM & TOURIST INFORMATION - Spiceball Park Road (canalside). Tel: 01295 753752. Small, but well-appointed museum. Open Mon-Sat, admission free. The well-stocked TIC is housed beside the canal in the Castle Quay shopping precinct. OX16 2PA

TOOLEY'S BOATYARD - canalside. Tel: 01295 272917. Iconic drydock. Gifts, chandlery, guided tours, blacksmith courses, and boat trips. OX16 2PQ

Connections
BUSES - services throughout the area. Stagecoach S4 runs along the Cherwell Valley. Tel: 0871 200 2233.

TRAINS - Chiltern, FGW and Cross Country services to/from Oxford, Leamington, London & Birmingham. Tel: 08457 484950.

TAXIS - A1 Taxis. Tel: 01295 272020.

A T Cropredy the Oxford Canal makes eye contact with the River Cherwell, but like all good bodice-rippers, the affair takes many twists and turns before consumation takes place. The canal company purchased Cropredy Mill and adapted the mill stream to provide the canal with water. Pass through the hole in the wall, brush past the nettles, and you'll come upon some of the old mill machinery and the water doing a disappearing trick beneath an old archway.

A new flood prevention scheme is evident in the vicinity of Bridge 159. By Hardwick Lock the M40 motorway makes its northernmost crossing of the canal. Below the lock the canal parallels the course of the Oxfordshire Ironstone Railway built by German prisoners of the First World War to access the ironstone quarries west of Banbury. Part of its trackbed, along with several miles of towpath, is included in the "Banbury Fringe Circular Walk".

Trade on the Oxford Canal petered out towards the end of the 1950s. Amongst the last regular cargoes were timber and tar. Up until this time Banbury supported its own canal community who were wont to congregate at a spit and sawdust pub called The Struggler. L. T. C. Rolt immortalised it in his *Inland Waterways of England*. The pub and the canal wharf were demolished in 1962 by the local council, who added insult to injury by building a bus station on the site. Now the whole area has been redeveloped into the Castle Quay Shopping Centre and Rolt may well be looking down from heaven and chuckling - with irony.

At least Tooley's drydock, also made famous by Rolt as the scene of *Cressy's* docking and refitting prior to the cruise of 1939 recounted in *Narrow Boat*, is preserved as part of the excellent Banbury Museum whose inland waterways gallery imaginatively and appropriately spans the canal.

Banbury squats like a bad bruise on the peaches and cream complexion of the Oxford Canal. For two or three turgid miles the picturesque images usually associated with this canal are invaded by ring-roads, factories and urban sprawl. But paradoxically, one can't help but feel grateful for a change of scene: all those meadows and wooded ridges can be a bit unremitting when encountered at three miles an hour. Banbury was the location, in 1955, of a campaigning boat rally to fight proposals to abandon the Oxford Canal. Seeing how busy the canal is now only serves to illustrate the folly of such short-sighted thinking.

⚠ Windlass required to operate lift bridge 164

19

Kings Sutton

Banbury

Heyford Wharf

Upper Heyford

Cropredy

Claydon Bottom

Rousham Eyecatcher

Cherwell Interludes

Oxford
Approaches

Isis Lock

Enslow

Duke's Cut

Bridge 242

St Barnabus, Jericho

PEMBROKE
OXFORD

ANGLO WELSH

21

DRAW bridges abound, their functional looks disguising the economy of construction inherent in their design. Most of them will be chained 'open' (reminding one, somewhat tangentially, of rolled-up shirtsleeves) and thus of no hindrance to boaters. Another worthwhile cost-cutting measure south of Banbury was the provision of single bottom gates for each lock chamber instead of the more usual mitred pairs: less call for acrobats at the locks!

The rocket-like spire of Kings Sutton church soars above the watermeadows, finding a photogenic mirror image in the canal from certain angles. The village boasts a railway station, but it is - along with other facilities - a bit of a hike away on the far side of the Cherwell, which forms the boundary between Oxon and Northants. Just south of Twyford Wharf the canal curves past a spill weir protected by concrete posts emblazoned with Oxford Canal Company initials.

Kings Sutton Lock is delightful. The keeper's cottage is simply built of brick with stone facing. On the opposite bank stands a former blacksmith's forge and stable block decorated by the addition of the village station's old name board. South of here the canal momentarily sheds its man-made character. The branches of pollarded willows hang caressingly over the water and poplars whisper in the breeze as a belt of woodland is encountered.

Into this exquisite landscape the M40 intrudes like a kick in the groin. When it was being constructed in the 1980s the *Sunday Times* ran a sequence of photographs looking out over the Cherwell Valley in the vicinity of Kings Sutton. It was a sobering illustration of the assassination of the Oxfordshire landscape. As hideous in its way as the sort of photographs they show of bodies in the streets after a military coup. As the Department of Transport used to boast, road schemes such as the M40 had their viability tested on a 'cost benefit basis'. Yes, we know: for the road lobby's benefit at the countryside's cost.

But how long before the motorway is outmoded like the canal itself and the now dismantled Banbury & Cheltenham Railway? The canal can be said to have functioned commercially for over a hundred and fifty years. The railway was relatively shortlived, opening in 1887 and closing to passengers in 1951, though surviving in goods use for another thirteen years. Its most celebrated train was the *Ports to Ports Express*, a service designed to effect the transfer of merchant seamen between Tyneside and South Wales. Did they, catching a glimpse of passing 'joshers', feel momentarily at home on their ten hour, landlocked journey?

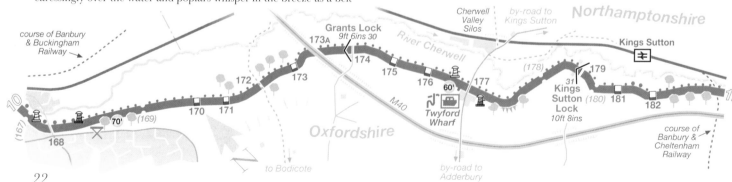

THE motorway bridge contrasts brutally with its neighbour, lift-bridge 183. It carries a dedication to a young civil engineering student fatally injured during construction of the road. Passing briefly into Northamptonshire, the canal shares much of this part of its journey with the adjoining railway, but loses little of its tranquillity in the process. Wharves past and present recall the canal's original purpose. The one at Aynho remains remarkably intact, its brick warehouse being home to a boatyard shop. Aynho's old railway station is of Brunellian design and dates from the inception of the original mixed gauge line between Oxford and Birmingham. When the Great Western Railway shaved twenty miles off their London to Birmingham route in 1910, Aynho marked the northern end of the 'cut off'. CART have a maintenance base at Nell Bridge.

Having played coquettishly with the canal's affections since Cropredy, the Cherwell acquires carnal knowledge by Aynho Weir Lock as the channel flows directly across the canal. The lock itself is shallow and diamond-shaped, Somerton being so deep that extra capacity had to be built into Aynho.

Somerton Deep Lock is, well, *very* deep. Overlooked by a rather over-shuttered cottage, it vies with Tardebigge on the Worcester & Birmingham for the honour of being the deepest narrowbeam chamber on the canal system. Certainly the steerer's eye view of things, when the lock is empty, is reminiscent of an elephant trap. Heaven knows how single-handed boat captains managed in the past. Tom Foxon hinted at his methods in *Number One*, also relating how it was his habit to swap lumps of coal with the lock-keeper in exchange for fresh laid eggs and rabbits.

Summary of Facilities

THE PIG PLACE - Adderbury (Nell Bridge). Tel: 0789 287 9447. Peripatetic boaters, the Wherrys (appropriate name) moored-up here in 2007 and haven't looked back. Still living afloat, they run this beguiling canalside small-holding specialising in pigs, poultry and sheep. The fruits of their labour of love are for sale - as are an esoteric range of facilities: overnight moorings with hook up; bottled gas, campsite, laundry room and hot tub hire! OX17 3NU

GREAT WESTERN ARMS - Aynho Wharf. Tel: 01869 338288. Congenial country pub - located between the canal and the old railway station and suitably decorated with memorabilia relating to both modes of transport. Hook Norton ales, bar and restaurant food, accommodation. OX17 3BP

AYNHO WHARF - Tel: 01869 338483. Small shop canalside selling gifts and basic groceries and newspapers. OX17 3BP

Down Somerton way the towpath becomes more of a gated footpath, a pleasant change for walkers, but cyclists can forget it!

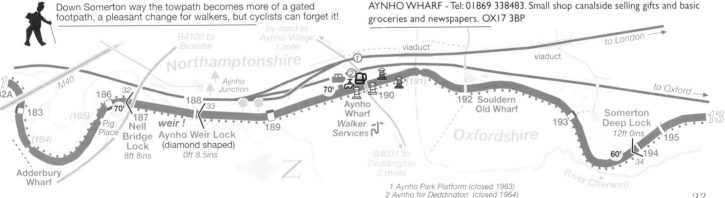

1 Aynho Park Platform (closed 1963)
2 Aynho for Deddington (closed 1964)

13 OXFORD CANAL The Heyfords 5mls/2lks/2hrs

CANAL, railway and river saunter companionably along the valley floor, but the roads keep cautiously to the shoulders of the hills. When the Cherwell bursts its banks, the escaping water forms an inland sea and wildfowl find this a conducive wintering ground. In spring the meadows seem full of lapwings carrying out their dizzy courtship; later, the sky is still filled with lark-song; one May morning we distinctly heard the trilling tones of a curlew.

From Somerton to Heyford the canal assumes the character of a river. The towpath loses its formality, becoming more of a track through the adjoining fields. Pollarded willows line the canal's banks, just as they do the Cherwell's, so that seen from a passing train, it is often difficult to tell immediately which is which. The water tower, prominent on a hillside to the east, belonged to RAF Upper Heyford, last used by the United States Airforce in 1993. The massive site which, in amongst all the military infrastructure, contained a hospital, supermarket and a large housing estate, remains earmarked for redevelopment.

Between the two Heyfords the canal arcs deliciously through a belt of woodland. There are glimpses of an attractive cluster of stone buildings - a church, manor house and 15th century tithe barn - below Allen's Lock.

Lower Heyford Mill ceased working at the end of the Second World War. The towpath has the air of an isthmus about it with the canal on one side and the river on the other. Lift-bridge 205 is said to have been built of iron to take the weight of the miller's traction engine. Nearby, a charmingly precarious tree house juts over the water.

Heyford Wharf is very similar to Aynho (Map 12), but on this occasion the warehouse is built of local stone. Nowadays it is in use as a vibrant hire base and offers useful additional facilities as well. A short walk from here lies Rousham House and its famous gardens, the work of William Kent. Kent's 'Rousham Eyecatcher' can be seen over the brow of the hill from Heyford Common lock or more closely from the paths which lead from bridges 203 or 205 towards the pretty hilltop village of Steeple Aston which makes for a pleasant walk across the river and the railway. There is an option to return via the road bridge over the Cherwell with views south to the imposing facade of Rousham House.

Barley Mow

Upper Heyford

Tithe Barn

River Cherwell

Lower Heyford

The Cleeves

204
36'
203
Allen's Lock
5ft 0ins
202
mill
The Bell
205
207
60'
14

Somerton
Fritwell & Somerton (csd 1964)
196
mill
(197)
199
198
200A
200
35'
Heyford Common Lock
7ft 2ins
Rousham Eyecatcher
Oxfordshire Narrowboats
206
B4030
Rousham House

12

Steeple Aston

Red Lion

for details of facilities at The Heyfords and Steeple Aston turn to page 26

24

THE Oxford Canal is arguably at its most charming and sublime between Heyford and Thrupp; drifting through the delectable landscape of the Cherwell Valley like something out of the slow, gorgeous heart of a concerto. At Northbrook the canal bridge abuts a much older structure spanning the river. This carried a packhorse route across the Cherwell centuries before the canal was even thought of. A mile or two to the south lies the course of the Romans' Akeman Street which linked Cirencester and St Albans.

The canal passes through an emerald tunnel of overhanging trees. In the heart of the woods lie the enigmatic ruins of an old cement works - now a bosky nature reserve. The canal formed the only practical access to and from the site. Coal, sand and gypsum were brought in by boat and cement taken out, much of it travelling only as far as Enslow where it was transhipped to rail. The works closed in 1927, production being transferred to a new plant - landmarked by a solitary chimney now - adjacent to Baker's Lock.

There used to be a pub called "The Three Pigeon's" by Bridge 213; hence the name of the adjoining lock. It must have been a welcome resort for the thirsty cement workers, but a long time has passed since the last pint was supped, though the building remains as a private residence, as does another of the Cherwell's former watermills. It's an idyllic quarter of an hour's walk from here - over sluice gates, millstreams and backwaters, and through waving fields of wheat and barley - to the not insubstantial village of Tackley. Enslow Marsh Sedgebed is a nature reserve islanded between the canal and the Cherwell.

Just beneath the railway bridge at Enslow you can see old mooring rings set in the wall and the scars of unloading apparatus where the cement was transhipped from boats into railway wagons. Smiths of Bletchington - a fourth generation aggregates company - operate a fleet of tipper lorries from premises adjoining Bridge 216; descendants once removed, one might assert, of the working narrowboats of the past. To the west, local residents appear to have outrageously exploited planning loopholes to improve satellite television reception. Below Baker's Lock the canal merges with the river and sharp bends (and capricious currents) abound on the sinuous, reed-fringed reach down to Shipton Weir Lock on Map 15.

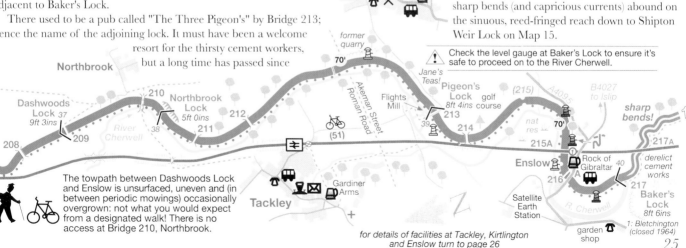

⚠️ Check the level gauge at Baker's Lock to ensure it's safe to proceed on to the River Cherwell.

The towpath between Dashwoods Lock and Enslow is unsurfaced, uneven and (in between periodic mowings) occasionally overgrown: not what you would expect from a designated walk! There is no access at Bridge 210, Northbrook.

for details of facilities at Tackley, Kirtlington and Enslow turn to page 26

25

The Heyfords   Map 13

Sisterly villages; 'Lower' being marginally the prettier.

Eating Drinking, Shopping etc

BARLEY MOW - Somerton Road, Upper Heyford. Tel: 01869 232300. Access from Allen's Lock. Plain but hospitable *Good Beer Guide* listed village local serving Fullers and food. Aunt Sally, an Oxfordshire pub game played with some intensity! OX25 5LB
THE BELL - Market Square, Lower Heyford. Tel: 01869 347176. Picturesque, creeper-clad inn overlooking the former market place. OX25 5NY
HEYFORD WHARF & KIZZIES BISTRO - Tel: 01869 340348. Boatyard based shop (gifts, provisions, wines and a nice line in Oxfordshire bottled beer), cafe/bistro, day boats, bike hire and self-catering accommodation. OX25 5PD

Connections

BUSES - Thames Travel 25A hourly Mon-Sat to/from Bicester and Oxford. Tel: 0871 200 2233. TRAINS - First Great Western services along the Cherwell Valley. Tel: 08457 484950.

Steeple Aston   Map 13

Charming hilltop village. The church is famous for its 14th century embroidered 'cope'; so rare that it's been appropriated by the V&A for safe-keeping!

Eating & Drinking

RED LION - South Side. Tel: 01869 340225. Attractive Hook Norton pub at far end of village open lunchtimes daily and evening Mon-Sat. OX25 4RY

Shopping

Well-stocked post office stores - Tel: 01869 340201.

Things to Do

ROUSHAM HOUSE & GARDENS - Tel: 01869 347110. Gardens open daily from 10am, last admission 4.30pm. No dogs or children under 15! OX25 4QU

Connections

BUSES - service S4 links Banbury with Oxford. Hourly Mon-Sat; four each way Sun. Tel: 0871 200 2233.

Tackley   Map 14

Quintessential 'Banburyshire' village. The church contains a memorial to forty-two locals who drowned on their way to a new life in Australia in 1845.

Eating & Drinking

GARDINER ARMS - Tackley. Tel: 01869 331266. Charming, wisteria-clad Greene King pub offering an excellent choice of food. Re-opened 2015. OX5 3AH

Shopping

Although it's a good 'country mile' away, you'll enjoy a visit to Tackley's volunteer run village shop and post office housed in the village hall and stocking a good range of locally produced farm foods, plus a 'self-service' coffee shop - Tel: 01869 331807.

Connections

BUSES - as Steeple Aston (ex Sun). TRAINS - as Heyford.

Kirtlington   Map 14

A mile's walk, along the Oxfordshire Way, from Pigeon's Lock brings you to this substantial village strung out along the Witney to Bicester main road. The Lamb Ale festival is a magnet for morris dancers.

Eating & Drinking

JANE'S TEAS - Mill Lane Farm (adjacent Pigeon's Lock). Tel: 0783 736 2683. Arcadian setting for light meals and teas open 1st and 3rd weekends Apr-Oct, noon to 5.30pm. Makeshift gazebos, wind chimes, aviaries and cakes magicked from freshly-laid eggs. Worth building your itinerary round. OX5 3HW
DASHWOOD HOTEL & RESTAURANT - South Green. Tel: 01869 352707. Boutique hotel and restaurant. Marlow Brewery ales. OX5 3HJ

OXFORD ARMS - Troy Lane. Tel: 01869 350208. Comfortable, stone-built pub adjoining the post office stores. OX5 3HA

Shopping

Post office stores with tea room - Tel: 01869 350356.

Connections

BUSES - Thames Travel 25A hourly Mon-Sat to/from Oxford and Bicester. Tel: 0871 200 2233.

Enslow   Map 14

ROCK OF GIBRALTAR - adjacent Bridge 216. Tel: 01869 331373. Famous old canalside pub with big waterside garden. Bar and restaurant food. OX5 3AY

Thrupp   Map 15

Picturesque canalside village. Walks over the watermeadows beside the Cherwell.

Eating & Drinking

THE BOAT - Thrupp. Tel: 01865 374279. Well-appointed country pub. A nice garden and a pretty pub sign. Greene King portfolio ales. OX5 1JY
ANNIE'S TEA ROOM - adjacent Bridge 221. Tel: 01865 842708. Salads, sandwiches and cream teas. Open 10am-5pm. Associated canoe and kayak hire. OX5 1JZ
JOLLY BOATMAN - canalside Bridge 223. Tel: 01865 377800. Main road pub popular with boaters. Greene King again. OX5 1JU

Kidlington   Map 15

Bloated village with the facilities of a town and the traffic to go with it. But there are some charming buildings from more innocent times.

Eating & Drinking

HIGHWAYMAN - Bridge 224. Tel: 01865 377388. Hotel/pub with pleasant canalside garden. Previously known as the Wise Alderman after a local railway signalman. Folk 3rd Sunday. OX5 1BF

15 OXFORD CANAL Thrupp & Kidlington 5mls/3lks/2hrs

A T Shipton Weir Lock canal and river part company, the Cherwell flowing south-eastwards past Islip to become that traditionally romantic stream of The Parks with its punts and its poets. Shipton Lock, like Aynho, is diamond shaped and not at all deep, but it can look as welcoming as a Cornish harbour in a gale when the navigable reach of the Cherwell is in spate. It is a remote spot, the old lock-keeper's cottage having been long ago demolished. Boaters from the local club at Thrupp (with superior - not to say intimate - knowledge of the shallows) employ the backwater for picnics.

The churches at Shipton and Hampton Gay repay a closer look. The former belongs to the Gothic Revival and is said to have been the inspiration behind Sandy Denny's haunting song *Bushes and Briars*. In the latter's graveyard a headstone commemorates Benjamin Taylor (19) of Wolverhampton, one of the thirty-four passengers who died in the Christmas Eve railway tragedy of 1874, when a derailed train plunged into the icy waters of the neighbouring canal. Deeper into Hampton Gay stand the eerie ruins of an Elizabethan manor house, uninhabited since a fire ravaged its interior in 1887. Stroll up and see it, by all means, but bear in mind that - as handwritten notices unequivocally put it: - 'the ruins *is* private'!

Shipton Manor (west of Bridge 220) was the home of William Turner, the Oxford watercolourist, at the beginning of the 19th century.

In the 1970s it was acquired by Richard Branson who turned it into a notable recording studio. The album which can be said to have launched the Virgin empire, Mike Oldfield's *Tubular Bells*, was recorded here.

Onomatopoetically not unlike the sound of a boat engine, Thrupp was once an important maintenance centre for the Oxford Canal. The former yard now houses a tea room and a canoe and kayak hire outlet. Set on a 90 degree bend, lift-bridge 221 is electrically operated, and you will require your Canal & River Trust facilities key to access the controls. A terrace of cottages fronts the canal as though it was a village street. This idyllic setting featured as the location for a grisly murder in the Inspector Morse mystery *The Riddle of the Third Mile*.

Thrupp might have become an important canal junction had 18th century proposals for a direct link between Hampton Gay and London ever got off the drawing board. The scheme was promoted in rivalry to the Grand Junction Canal and came about largely because of the poor state of the Thames at the time. In the event, the Grand Junction received its Royal Assent first and the London & Western Canal, as it was to be known, languished, its subscribers receiving only sixpence back in the pound on their misplaced investment and optimism.

There are OCC gate posts at former canal employee cottages by Bridge 224. Thence the canal skirts the built-up - but unobtrusive - housing zones of the much-expanded 'village' of Kidlington.

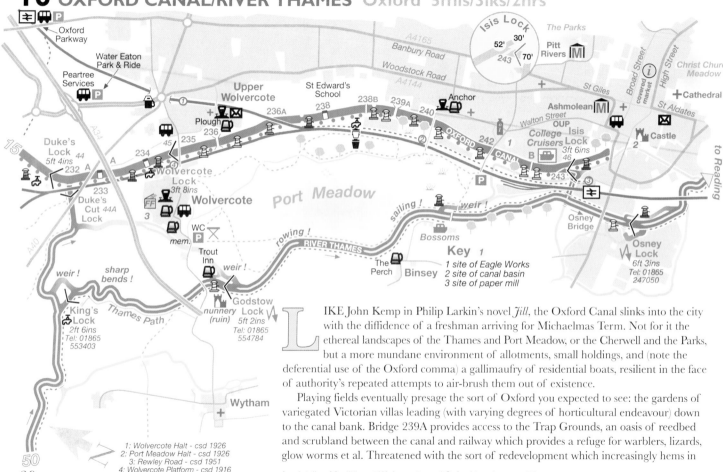

Oxford Parkway

Water Eaton Park & Ride

Peartree Services

Oxford Parkway

A4165
Banbury Road
Woodstock Road
A4144

The Parks

Isis Lock
52' 30'
243 70'

Pitt Rivers

Upper Wolvercote

St Edward's School

Plough

236A 238 238B 239A 240

Anchor

Broad Street
High Street
St Giles
Walton Street
St Aldates

Ashmolean

Christ Church Meadow

covered market

Cathedral

Castle

OXFORD CANAL

242 1
College Cruisers
OUP
Isis Lock
3ft 6ins
46
B 243

45 235 236
234
232 A
233
Duke's Lock 5ft 4ins 44
A
Duke's Cut 44A Lock

15

Wolvercote Lock 3ft 8ins

Wolvercote

mem.
WC

Trout Inn

Port Meadow

sailing ! weir !

rowing !

RIVER THAMES

Bossoms

The Perch Binsey

Key 1
1 site of Eagle Works
2 site of canal basin
3 site of paper mill

Osney Bridge

Osney Lock
6ft 3ins
Tel: 01865 247050

to Reading

weir ! sharp bends !

King's Lock
2ft 6ins
Tel: 01865 553403

Thames Path

weir !

Godstow Lock
5ft 2ins
Tel: 01865 554784

nunnery (ruin)

Wytham

1: Wolvercote Halt - csd 1926
2: Port Meadow Halt - csd 1926
3: Rewley Road - csd 1951
4: Wolvercote Platform - csd 1916

50
28

L IKE John Kemp in Philip Larkin's novel *Jill*, the Oxford Canal slinks into the city with the diffidence of a freshman arriving for Michaelmas Term. Not for it the ethereal landscapes of the Thames and Port Meadow, or the Cherwell and the Parks, but a more mundane environment of allotments, small holdings, and (note the deferential use of the Oxford comma) a gallimaufry of residential boats, resilient in the face of authority's repeated attempts to air-brush them out of existence.

Playing fields eventually presage the sort of Oxford you expected to see: the gardens of variegated Victorian villas leading (with varying degrees of horticultural endeavour) down to the canal bank. Bridge 239A provides access to the Trap Grounds, an oasis of reedbed and scrubland between the canal and railway which provides a refuge for warblers, lizards, glow worms et al. Threatened with the sort of redevelopment which increasingly hems in

for details of facilities at Wolvercote and Oxford turn to page 30

on other parts of the canal, the Trap Grounds' supporters had to appeal as high as the House of Lords to ensure its survival. No one succeeded in preserving Lucy's Eagle Works for posterity. Perhaps no one even tried. The once cacophonous foundry site has been covered by balconied apartments. But there will be those, like us, who mourn the sense of activity it brought to this end of the canal before closure in 2005. Incidentally, the last traffic regularly carried by canal boat to Oxford was coal for Morrell's Brewery, and the curtain came down on that in 1961.

The Italianate tower of St Barnabus' church overlooks designated visitor moorings, and its sonorous chime will invade your beauty-sleep. Betjeman wrote of its "tubular bells" and "polychromatical lacing of bricks". The terraced streets of Jericho (scene of another Morse murder enquiry) are fronted by the boatyard of College Cruisers.

An elegant cast iron bridge spans the entrance to Isis Lock as the main line of the canal heads for its quiet oblivion, a couple of hundred yards or so further on. Once upon a time the Oxford Canal terminated more grandiloquently in a broad basin of busy wharves overlooked by the castle keep. Business was brisk in coal brought down the cut from Warwickshire, and Temple Thurston came here in search of Eynsham Harry*. But in 1937 the site was acquired by Lord Nuffield for the erection of a new college in his name. Since then the Oxford Canal has not so much terminated as petered out (although there are vague proposals to recreate the terminus) and, as all but the last few yards are largely occupied by residential boats, the visiting boater has little alternative but to moor somewhere back between bridges 239A and 243.

Winding needs to be considered as well: boats of 30ft or less can just about turn at the very end of the canal; 52ft and under can turn in the winding hole by Bridge 243; anything longer than that and you'll have to go down through Isis Lock into one of the Thames' backwaters to turn. Having got that far, it is difficult to resist the temptation to find your way out of Oxford via the Thames and Duke's Cut. To do this you'll need a Thames short period registration acquired from the keeper at Osney or Godstow locks. Proceed along the Sheepwash Channel (where, sadly,

* The Flower of Gloster by E. Temple Thurston - 1911.

the yeoman of Oxfordshire no longer gather to dip their flocks) and pass beneath the railway; noticing, as you do, the rusty remains of a railway swing-bridge which used to carry the line to the old London & North Western terminus on Rewley Road. Beyond the railway the channel emerges to join the Thames itself. You should turn right, upstream in the direction of Binsey, and Godstow Lock. A left turn would take you downstream towards Reading, as enthusiastically embraced by *Pearson's Canal Companion to the Kennet & Avon and River Thames*.

The next reach is spellbinding. Soon the tree-lined banks open out to expose the full extent of Port Meadow where cattle and horses graze against a skyline of Oxford's dreaming spires. Gerard Manley Hopkins wrote a poem called *Binsey Poplars* in memory of some aspens which had lined the riverbank until they were cut down in 1879: 'All felled, felled, all are felled' the poem laments; an act of arboreal vandalism - it doesn't take an A Level student of English Literature to infer - he bitterly opposed.

Godstow Lock returns you from the realms of Parnassus. It's worth mooring to the grassy bank upstream of Godstow's ancient stone bridge to explore the ruins of the nunnery where Henry II's mistress, Fair Rosamund, died. You do so in the footsteps of L. T. C. Rolt who, gathering material for his Festival of Britain potboiler *The Thames from Mouth to Source*, skinny-dipped at midnight. You may still hear him splashing about.

The Thames - archaically known as Isis hereabouts - meanders from Godstow to King's Lock, the first, heading upstream, to remain unmechanised. To regain the canal you must turn right above the lock. The main channel proceeds upstream to Lechlade as described on Maps 45-50. The Duke's Cut was actually the original link between the canal and the river, being opened in 1789. It was owned by the Duke of Marlborough, hence the name. Boats also used it to gain access to a paper mill at Wolvercote, which relied on Warwickshire coal until 1951. For many years the mill was owned by the Oxford University Press and specialised in the sort of wafer-thin paper used in the production of prayer books. All too soon, passing beneath the A40 and the railway, the little Duke's Cut Lock returns you to the Oxford Canal; rather better for the experience, it has to be said.

Oxford
Map 16

Why can't everywhere be like Oxford? Imbued with wisdom and beauty. Inhabited by a populace set on a path of self-fulfilment. A framework for humanity nonpareil. Like a supermarket trolley-dash, you have forty-eight hours at the visitor moorings to allow as much of it to rub off on you as is possible.

Eating & Drinking

THE ANCHOR - Hayfield Road (Bridge 240). Tel: 01865 510282. Refurbished suburban pub within easy reach of the canal. Open daily from 9am (10am Suns). Wide choice of food and Wadsworth ales. OX2 6TT
BRASSERIE BLANC - Walton Street. Tel: 01865 510999. Resilient Raymond B. restaurant. OX2 6AG
BROWNS - Woodstock Road. Tel: 01865 511995. An Oxford institution housed in an old Morris garage. Open from 8.30am (9am Suns). OX2 6HA
NOSEBAG - St Michael's Street. Tel: 01865 721033. Long-established wholefood cafe restaurant. Open from 9.30am daily. A Pearson perennial! OX1 2DU
OLD BOOKBINDERS ALE HOUSE - Victor Street. Tel: 01865 553549. Pub adjacent canal in Jericho which derives its name from its proximity to the Oxford University Press. Closed Mons. OX2 6BT
THE PERCH - Binsey Lane. Tel: 01865 728891. Renovated (2015) 17th century inn close to the riverbank. Open from 10.30am daily. OX2 0NG
TURL STREET KITCHEN - Turl Street. Tel: 01865 264171. Informal, inexpensive, inspired. OX1 3DH
COTE BRASSERIE - George Street. Tel: 01865 251992. Reliable chain open 8am (9am Sat & Sun). OX1 2BE
THE RICKETY PRESS - Cranham Street, Jericho. Tel: 01865 424851. Gastropub within easy reach of canal moorings. Open from noon daily. OX2 6DE
ZHENG - Walton Street. Tel: 01865 558888. Acclaimed Malaysian restaurant. OX2 6EA

Shopping

Drawing on a wide range of custom and taste, Oxford's shops are inspired to an admirable eclecticism. The Covered Market (off High Street) hosts the most wonderful cross-section of retailers. Walton Street (easily accessed from bridges 242 and 242B provides a microcosm of Oxford in its own right and features many interesting shops and eating establishments.

Things to Do

TOURIST INFORMATION - Broad Street. Tel: 01865 686430. OX1 3AS
CITY SIGHTSEEING OXFORD - open top bus rides with running commentary. Regular departures from the railway station (OX1 1HS) and city centre stops. Tel: 01865 790522.
ASHMOLEAN MUSEUM - Beaumont Street. Tel: 01865 278002. Britain's oldest public museum displaying European, Egyptian and Near Eastern antiquities. Closed Mons. Free admission. OX1 2PH
PITT RIVERS MUSEUM - South Parks Road. Tel: 01865 270927. Anthropology and archaeology. OX1 3PP
CARFAX TOWER - Carfax. 99 steps to heaven for a bird's eye view of the city of dreaming spires.
PUNT HIRE - Oxford's most traditional means of seduction (and indeed various other types of self-propelled craft) can be hired from boat houses at Folly Bridge (Tel: 01865 243421 - OX1 4LA) on the Thames and Magdalen Bridge (Tel: 01865 202643 - OX1 4AX) on the Cherwell.
COLLEGES - over thirty colleges make up Oxford University. Many of them are world famous such as Balliol and Merton which are both of 13th century origin; Magdalen (pronounced 'Maudlin') which dates from 1458; and Christ Church founded in 1525 by Cardinal Wolsey. The general (less well-educated) public may look around most of them in the afternoons.

OPEN SPACES - much of Oxford's charm rests in the proliferation of green spaces, the city's lungs. These include: The Parks, Christ Church Meadow and Port Meadow. A stroll - or a picnic - on any of them comes as a refreshing experience after the hurly-burly of the main thoroughfares and helps put Oxford in the context of its riverside setting.

Connections

TRAINS - First Great Western local services along the Cherwell Valley to/from Banbury. Frequent services to/from London Paddington. Tel: 08457 484950.
BUSES - Service S4 runs up the Cherwell Valley to Banbury, hourly Mon-Sat and four times each way on Suns. Stagecoach service 18 shadows the Thames northwards and westwards from Oxford at hourly intervals Mon-Sat. Tel: 0871 200 2233.

Wolvercote
Map 16

Residential suburb situated between the canal and the Thames and the edge of Port Meadow. The paper mill closed in 1998 and still awaits redevelopment. A memorial plaque at the western edge of the village commemorates two airmen killed in 1912.

Eating & Drinking

THE TROUT - Godstow Road. Tel: 01865 510930. Famous old pub in idyllic setting above Godstow Lock. Open daily from 11am, food from noon. OX2 8PN
Three other pubs and a Chinese takeaway.

Shopping

Convenience store in the centre of the village equidistant between the canal and the river. There is additionally a Londis store/post office in Upper Wolvercote easily accessed from bridges 235/6

Connections

BUSES - Oxford Bus Co. service 6 operates every 15 minutes (20 mins on Suns) to/from the city centre. Tel: 01865 785400.

Bridge 43

Grand Union Canal

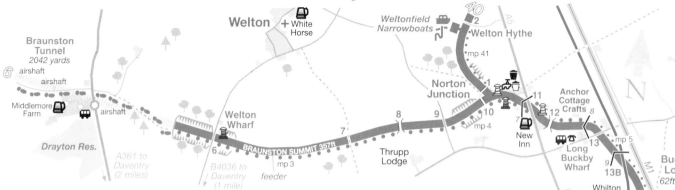

NORTON JUNCTION marks the point at which the Leicester Section of the Grand Union network diverges from the main London-Birmingham line and heads off on its cross country hike towards the famous locks at Foxton. The picturesque little toll house which overlooks the junction was the base, for many years, of the late Commander Fielding of the Salvation Army. In the Fifties he and his wife ran the mission boats *Salvo* and *Aster*, cruising around the canal system, ministering to the needs of the working boat families.

West of Norton Junction the Braunston Summit (one of three between London and Birmingham) essays its short, partially subterranean course between the lock flights at Braunston and Buckby. The scenery hereabouts is typical of the Northamptonshire Uplands. To the south can be seen the spire of Daventry's parish church, to the north, Welton's tower.

Being only three miles long, the provision of an adequate water supply was (and remains) of paramount importance. Two reservoirs, Drayton and Daventry (great names for a pair of private detectives), go some way to meeting this need, whilst there are also pumps at the foot of each flight which help by returning water to the summit. Daventry District Council have produced ambitious plans for a brand new canal arm to provide a fresh focus for tourism in the town.

Braunston Tunnel is the seventh longest currently navigable. There is no towpath through it, but narrowboats can pass inside. Until the mid Thirties a steam tug service hauled unpowered boats through the tunnel. The brickwork was extensively repaired and replaced in 1979 and again between 1985-8, but somehow the soot from the tugs still clings to the older lining. Walkers make their way over the top of the tunnel by way of the old horse path, an enjoyable adventure in its own right.

South of Norton Junction lie Buckby Locks. Buckby is well known throughout the waterways as the home of the 'Buckby Can'. These metal water carriers, adorned with 'roses & castles', were an essential piece of the boat families' inventory, because their boats were not equipped with water tanks and running water from the tap. Watling Street crosses the canal at Long Buckby Wharf and here the towpath changes sides. A pedestrian tunnel lengthens the odds of negotiating the A5 in one piece.

For a couple of miles the canal is in close proximity to the M1 motorway and correspondingly loses much of its inherent peace and quiet. The ghosts in this landscape must be severely disturbed, but ghosts there must be, for the Roman settlement of Bannaventa stood adjacent to what is now Whilton Marina, and the medieval village of Muscott lay to the east of Bridge 18. An enjoyable circular walk can be essayed between bridges 18 and 21 (Map 18) by going east of the canal from either of these points, crossing the hideously noisy motorway and taking the gated by-road which passes prettily through the grounds of the Brockhall estate.

Buckby Wharf   Map 17

The New Inn (Tel: 01327 844747 - NN6 7PW) by Buckby Top Lock opens from noon daily and is popular with motorists and boaters alike. A few hundred yards down the towpath stands Anchor Cottage Crafts (Tel: 01327 842140 - NN6 7PP) a charming little canal shop.

Connections

BUSES - Stagecoach service 11 operates approximately hourly to/from Daventry and Long Buckby Mon-Sat. Tel: 0871 200 2233.

TRAINS - Long Buckby station lies a mile to the east of Buckby Wharf and is served by trains between Northampton and Birmingham. Tel: 08457 484950.

Whilton   Map 17

Canalside community at the foot of Buckby Locks. Garden centre, tea rooms, farm shop and pottery. Small selection of provisions and cafe at Whilton Marina.

Muscott   Map 17

HEART OF THE SHIRES - west of Bridge 18. Tel: 01604 230213. Shopping 'village' of specialist outlets (including a tea room and a deli) housed in what was a Victorian 'model' farm. Open 10am-5pm daily. NN7 4LB

Weedon Bec   Map 18

Legend has it that Weedon's cornfields were being raped by flocks of geese until St Werburgh brought one of their number back to life, hence the shape of the weather vane on St Peter's ochre-coloured church, in the shadow of the canal embankment. One of the graves marks the resting place of Alice Old who lived long enough in the 17th Century to be ruled over by seven sovereigns. Down from Bridge 24 you'll come upon a cornucopia of antique shops, but the quieter core of Weedon lies to the west, well away from the A5, where the vast barracks may be seen.

Eating & Drinking

THE CROSSROADS - Watling Street. Tel: 01327 340354. Chef & Brewer pub/restaurant/hotel open from 11am daily (noon Sun). NN7 4BX

HEART OF ENGLAND - High Street. Tel: 01327 340335. This imposing Marston's 'Two for One' pub/restaurant/hotel was originally constructed in the 18th century as a farmhouse. NN7 4QD

THE NARROWBOAT - Watling Street. Tel: 01327 340536. Charles Wells pub offering food and motel style accommodation alongside Bridge 26. NN7 4RZ

THE PLUME OF FEATHERS - Market Square. Tel: 01327 340978. Village-centre local. NN7 4QU

WEEDON HOUSE - High Street. Tel: 01327 349388. Chinese takeaway. NN7 4QD

Shopping

The village shops are located west of the canal and ideally - not to say idyllically - reached from the offside visitor moorings on the embankment, down steps and through the churchyard. The shops include a 'One-Stop' convenience store (open 6am-10pm daily), post office, greengrocer and a pharmacy. A Tesco Express (6am-11pm) has opened at the crossroads.

Connections

BUSES - Stagecoach service D3 operates hourly Mon-Sat (bi-hourly Sun) to/from Northampton and Daventry. Tel: 0871 200 2233.

TAXIS - Weedon Taxis. Tel: 01327 341007.

Nether Heyford   Map 18

Half a mile to east of canal with sizeable green. Nice parish church of St Peter & St Paul tucked away to rear of houses.

Eating & Drinking

FORESTERS ARMS - The Green. Tel: 01327 340622. Village local. NN7 3LE

OLDE SUN - Middle Street. Tel: 01327 340164. Charming pub characterised by enamelled advertisements and vintage machinery. NN7 3LL

Shopping

One-Stop convenience store (open 6am-10pm daily), and butcher called Heyford Meats.

Connections

BUSES - Stagecoach service D3 operates hourly Mon-Sat (bi-hourly Sun) to/from Northampton and Daventry (via Weedon). Tel: 0871 200 2233.

18 GRAND UNION CANAL Weedon 5mls/0lks/2hrs

WHEN Napoleon was busy acquiring as much of Europe as he could early in the 19th century, the Government got out a map of England and looked for somewhere safe to hide King George III. Their eye fell upon the tiny Northamptonshire village of Weedon Bec which, not entirely coincidentally, had just been linked to London with the completion of William Jessop's Grand Junction Canal. Here they built barracks and a Royal Pavilion. A canal arm led off the main line, entering the barracks through a portcullis. It was obviously intended that Weedon would be defended to the last. Happily, Bonaparte met his match elsewhere, and the King never needed to use his splendid pavilion. But the barracks remained in use for many years and, on occasions, troops were carried by canal boat from here to trouble spots and ports of embarkation. At one time the depot was home to the Army Equitation School.

A fifteen mile pound separates the lock flights at Buckby and Stoke Bruerne. To maintain this horizontality, the canal accommodates the undulations of the countryside: wrapping itself around the sinuous valley of the upper Nene, and crossing the river by way of a high embankment at Weedon.

The Nene, one of England's most unsung, yet delightful rivers, rises near the village

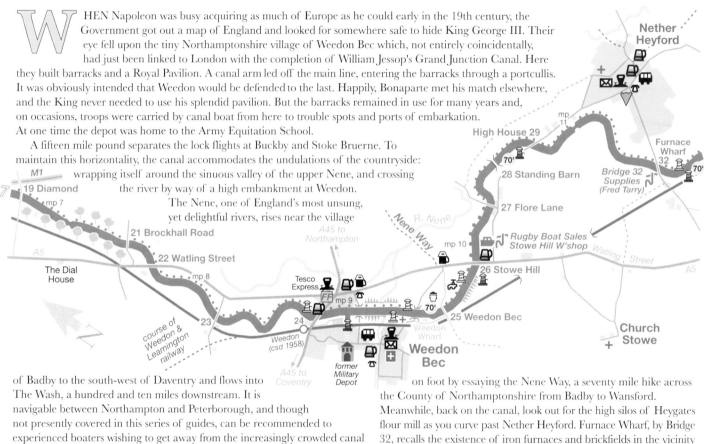

of Badby to the south-west of Daventry and flows into The Wash, a hundred and ten miles downstream. It is navigable between Northampton and Peterborough, and though not presently covered in this series of guides, can be recommended to experienced boaters wishing to get away from the increasingly crowded canal network. Alternatively you can savour the river's considerable beauty

on foot by essaying the Nene Way, a seventy mile hike across the County of Northamptonshire from Badby to Wansford. Meanwhile, back on the canal, look out for the high silos of Heygates flour mill as you curve past Nether Heyford. Furnace Wharf, by Bridge 32, recalls the existence of iron furnaces and brickfields in the vicinity during the 19th Century.

19 GRAND UNION CANAL Gayton Junction 4.5mls/0lks/1.5hrs

THE landscape pitches and rolls like a sea swell as mileposts count the distance to or from Braunston. Their initials - G. J. C. Co. - are *initially* mystifying ... shouldn't that J be a U? But this canal was built as the Grand Junction, the name Grand Union only coming into play in the 1930s following a series of amalgamations on the route between London and Birmingham. One doesn't think of the Grand Union as a pretty canal - it is too businesslike and muscular for that - but its remote journeying across the Shires has the reposeful quality of a postprandial stroll after a Sunday roast. At least that's how it feels for today's pleasure boaters, doubtless the working boatmen of the past were too preoccupied with 'getting 'em ahead' to pay homage to the countryside's charm. But if the neighbouring trains emphasise the modern urge to be elsewhere, the canal acclimatizes you kindly to each new view. The passengers in those sleek Pendolinos may be alighting at Euston before you get to Gayton, but people who go to great lengths to save time usually end up by having to kill it. Incidentally, the lack of freight trains doesn't mean that the M1 has finally robbed all commercial activity from the canal and the railway, it's simply that most of the goods goes the long way round through Northampton. 'Banbury Lane' - which links Banbury with Northampton - was once a drover's road, but its origins may go back to prehistoric times. In the heyday of the canal there was a wharf and tavern here. The buildings - three storeys with an attic - are typical of the architectural style of the Grand Junction

for details of facilities at Bugbrooke turn to page 37

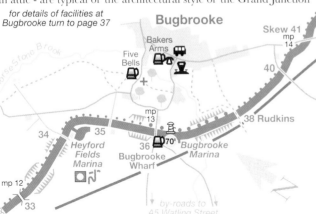

for details of facilities at Gayton turn to page 37

company, and similar structures can be seen at many wharves along this section of the canal. As trade evaporated, most of the canal pubs lost their licences and were converted into private residences, a trend still sadly echoed to this day. As part of a scheme to eradicate level crossings on the upgraded West Coast Main Line railway, a new canal bridge has been added alongside the original bridge number 43. Similarly, the footpath which crosses the canal at Bridge 38 has been expensively provided with a footbridge over the railway. Goodness knows how it comes to be so heavily graffitied in these rural climes. At Gayton Junction the Northampton Arm branches off from the main line and commences its whirlwind descent to the River Nene.

19A GRAND UNION CANAL Northampton 5mls/17lks/4hrs

IF the Scriptures imply that a hard-working life will land you in Heaven, the Northampton Arm's heavily-locked descent to the celestial Nene is the inland waterways' proof-of-the-pudding. But first there is the little matter of purgatory in the shape of seventeen frustratingly narrow locks; frustrating, in the sense that, had they been built to the same gauge as the main line, Birmingham might have boasted a wide-beam link with the North Sea. Of such shortcomings is history shaped. How often the inland navigator comes upon restrictions in beam and draught which have

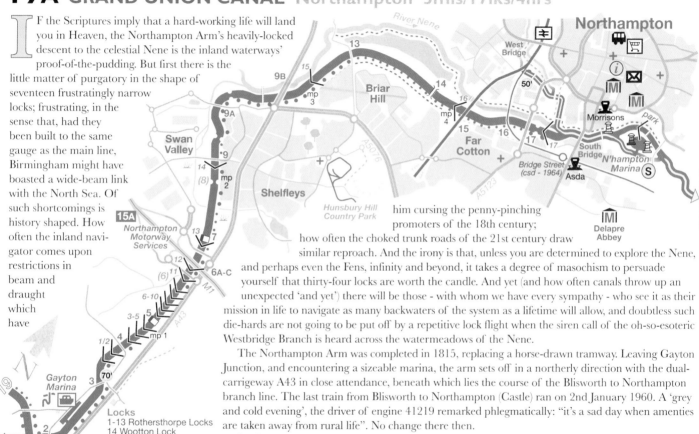

him cursing the penny-pinching promoters of the 18th century; how often the choked trunk roads of the 21st century draw similar reproach. And the irony is that, unless you are determined to explore the Nene, and perhaps even the Fens, infinity and beyond, it takes a degree of masochism to persuade yourself that thirty-four locks are worth the candle. And yet (and how often canals throw up an unexpected 'and yet') there will be those - with whom we have every sympathy - who see it as their mission in life to navigate as many backwaters of the system as a lifetime will allow, and doubtless such die-hards are not going to be put off by a repetitive lock flight when the siren call of the oh-so-esoteric Westbridge Branch is heard across the watermeadows of the Nene.

The Northampton Arm was completed in 1815, replacing a horse-drawn tramway. Leaving Gayton Junction, and encountering a sizeable marina, the arm sets off in a northerly direction with the dual-carriageway A43 in close attendance, beneath which lies the course of the Blisworth to Northampton branch line. The last train from Blisworth to Northampton (Castle) ran on 2nd January 1960. A 'grey and cold evening', the driver of engine 41219 remarked phlegmatically: "it's a sad day when amenties are taken away from rural life". No change there then.

Just in case you've got cold feet, a winding-hole precedes the top lock. Thereafter, the arm quite literally, takes the plunge, chamber following chamber* in a hell-bent dash beneath the M1. Quaint

Some of the locks are fitted with anti-vandal attachments requiring a CART facilities key to release.

Locks
1-13 Rothersthorpe Locks
14 Wootton Lock
15 Hardingstone Lock
16 Hunsbury Lock
17 Northampton Lock

draw-bridges punctuate your progress, but never appear to require lifting; indeed one of them has been reduced to a kit of parts. The arm passes beneath the motorway in a concrete vault, where local adolescents display the creative urge of cavemen. In the early days of the motorway - opened in 1959 - this crossing regularly witnessed anachronistic encounters between working narrowboats and hurtling lorries, for the arm remained in commecial use for another ten years with boats carrying grain to a mill on the River Nene at Wellingborough.

Below Lock 13 the canal used to find itself in a wetland landscape of meadows, reedbeds and willows. But in recent years, Northampton's burgeoning housing estates and business parks have broken the spell. The National Lift Tower forms a lofty landmark. Erected in 1982 and closed in 1997, it has experienced - how can we put it? - highs and lows. Demolition, preservation? - it became the subject of heated local debate. In the event, it was recommissioned in 2009, as a useful resource for lift manufacturers and companies requiring vertical space for testing; such as certain elements of the media, determined to calibrate just how far and how fast they could sink.

Between locks 14 and 15 bridge numbering appears to have gone awry in recent years: 9B leaping to 13 without blinking. Towards the end of its now nostalgically admired existence, British Waterways dispatched teams of innumerate contractors out with instructions to attach bridge plates to any inanimate structures they encountered. A&E departments reportedly overflowed with BW's in-house maintenance teams.

The arm, cosmetically enhanced by volunteers from the Northampton Branch of the IWA, bears eastwards. To the south rises Hunsbury Hill, site of an ironworks to which ore and stone was ferried by boat from Blisworth. Lock 16 is overlooked by a busy railway line as the arm commences its last lap. Bridge 16 carries the rusty track of a chord which linked Northampton's Castle and Bridge stations. Plaques celebrate the completion, in 2000, of the town's improved flood defences. And then, overlooked by Carlsberg's Lego-like brewery, the arm ends at Lock 17. Many boats will need to descend into the river to turn, at which point you're on Environment Agency waters, and should be armed with an appropriate licence, obtainable from Gayton Marina. Upstream, you can delve into the shallow delights of the Westbridge Arm. Downstream lies ... well, the 'Nen' and nirvana. Bon voyage, one of these days, fingers crossed, we'll find sufficient space to accompany you again.

Northampton   Map 19A

'More like Belgium than any other town I know in England' said the late architectural writer and broadcaster, Ian Nairn (see maps 33/7) and you only have to look at the Guildhall and the Market Place to see immediately what he meant. And they are just the tip of an iceberg in an underrated county town humming with handsome buildings from many eras. Would that we had space to pay homage, but personal favourites include: St Peter's (lovingly cared for by the Churches Conservation Trust) on Marefair; 78 Derngate (designed by Charles Rennie Mackintosh for the model-maker Bassett-Lowke); and Latimer & Crick's riverside warehouse which provides an attractive counterpoint to South Bridge. Enjoy!

Bugbrooke   Map 19

Bugbrooke boasts some immensely attractive streets of ochre coloured houses, once upon a time it was known as a centre for ladder-making. Handsome church. Bugbrooke Mill, a mile to the north on the banks of the Nene, produces flour and animal feeds for Heygates.

Eating & Drinking

THE WHARF - Bridge 36. Tel: 01604 832585. Purpose-built canalside pub offering bar and restaurant food. Large waterside garden. Frog Island beers from Northampton. NN7 3QB

FIVE BELLS - Tel: 01604 831618. Pleasantly refurbished country pub famed for its steaks. NN7 3PB
Third pub, called the Bakers Arms, in the village.

Shopping

Convenience store 6am-8pm ex Sun (6.30am-4pm).

Connections

BUSES - Stagecoach service D3 operates hourly Mon-Sat (bi-hourly Sun) to/from Northampton and Daventry (via Weedon). Tel: 0871 200 2233.

Gayton   Map 19

Quiet hilltop village of mellow ochre-coloured stone.

Eating & Drinking

QUEEN VICTORIA - High Street. Tel: 01604 858878. 'Country pub & dining'. Charles Wells and Hook Norton. Closed Mons, and Sun eves. B&B. NN7 3HD
EYKYN ARMS - High Street. Tel: 01604 858361. Cosy Greene King local. NN7 3HD

20 GRAND UNION CANAL Stoke Bruerne 4mls/2lks/2hrs

BLISWORTH and Stoke Bruerne are contrasting canalside communities separated by the third* longest presently navigable tunnel in Britain. The first attempt at a tunnel, commenced in 1793, was abandoned three years later due to instabilities in the ground. In the meantime cargoes were being transhipped across the hill; firstly by horse and cart, subsequently via a tramway employing L-shaped rails. A second attempt at tunnelling, on a different alignment, was successfully opened in 1805, its completion confirming the fulfilment of the Grand Junction Canal.

Blisworth Tunnel's dimensions permitted narrowboats to pass inside, but no towpath was provided. At the outset boats were poled through, rather in the manner of Oxford punts, but this practice was apparently abandoned in favour of the more traditional art of 'legging', though with, not surprisingly, a considerable number of fatalities. The canal company provided registered leggers who wore brass arm bands proclaiming their role. Later, as traffic increased, a steam tug service was provided, and although this was withdrawn as long ago as 1936, there is still a reek and an aroma of soot and steam to be savoured within the tunnel's confines. Bridge 50 is known as Candle Bridge, recalling that in far off days the lady who lived in a nearby cottage sold tallow candles to the leggers.

In the late 1970s, in common with many other impressive canal structures, Blisworth Tunnel was feeling its age, and suffering from a backlog of indifferent maintenance. Its lining deteriorated to such an extent that it became necessary to close the tunnel for four years, effectively severing the canals of the Midlands from those of the South-East. £4 million was spent on relining the bore, and the tunnel re-opened in 1984.

The Grand Union skirts Blisworth, passing beneath the A43 and the West Coast Main Line in the process. This area was once riddled with iron stone quarries linked by tramway to loading stages along the canal bank, much of the stone being carried the comparatively short distance by boat to Hunsbury Hill Furnaces on the Northampton Arm. Blisworth railway station was the junction for the Stratford & Midland Junction Railway (see page 17) as well as the line from Blisworth to Peterborough which used, picturesquely, to accompany much of the course of the River Nene.

Blisworth Mill, a handsome brick building once used as a depot by the Grand Union Canal Carrying Company - but now, perhaps inevitably, converted into housing - overlooks Bridge 51. Blisworth Tunnel's northern portal is built from blue brick. Half an hour after entering the tunnel you can compare this with the redbrick of the southern portal. Here, two small buildings provide reminders of the canal's working days: one was used as

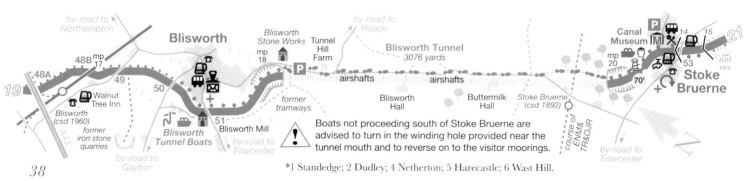

Boats not proceeding south of Stoke Bruerne are advised to turn in the winding hole provided near the tunnel mouth and to reverse on to the visitor moorings.

*1 Standedge; 2 Dudley; 4 Netherton; 5 Harecastle; 6 Wast Hill.

38

a bunkering and maintenance shed for the tunnel tugs; the other was a stable. Blacksmith, Bob Nightingale, uses the former as a smithy.

Where Blisworth dreams, Stoke Bruerne bristles, both with boaters and tourists, the latter attracted here primarily by the village's famous Canal Museum. Steerers should handle their craft with consideration and courtesy, keeping a special eye open for the trip boats which ply between the winding hole and the top lock. As the cutting recedes, the canal narrows through the site of Rectory Bridge, then widens as it reaches the wharf and associated buildings which, taken as a whole, make Stoke Bruerne such an iconic canal location. A three-storey, stone built mill dominates the wharf. Once it ground corn with machinery driven by steam, now it houses the celebrated museum, first opened to the inquisitive public as long ago as 1963. A basin for boats delivering coal to the mill lay behind where the tall poplar trees now stand, and all trace has vanished of a roving bridge which carried the towpath over the entrance to this dock. A row of stone cottages originally provided for millworkers - but later used by canal employees - separates the mill from a brick house of Georgian style. This was for many years a shop catering for the needs of boating families. But in the twilight days of commercial carrying it was the home of Stoke's favourite daughter, Sister Mary Ward, a lady of high ideals and humility, who took it upon herself to look after the boat people in sickness and in health until her retirement in 1962. Buildings on the west bank of the canal include the wharfinger's office and house, now occupied by canal author and water transport campaigner, David Blagrove. David's book, *Bread Upon the Waters*, paints a vivid description of life on the Grand Union Canal towards the end of commercial carrying in the 1960s. The disused lock on the west side was part of the original flight of 1804. The canal was so busy that these were briefly duplicated thirty years later. But by the 1850s, in the face of railway competition, the earlier locks fell out of use. All part of the charm and fascination of Stoke Bruerne!

Blisworth   Map 20

Church and Baptist chapel dominate the view from the canal, and there are some fine looking stone buildings, reminders of the village's significance as a centre of quarrying. On the road which runs across the hill in parallel to the tunnel's subterranean course, stands a building bearing the inscription: "Blisworth Stone Works".

Eating & Drinking

WALNUT TREE INN - Station Road. Tel: 01604 859551. Former 19th century station hotel smartly refurbished. Bar and restaurant food, real ales and accommodation. NN7 3DS

ROYAL OAK - Chapel Lane. Tel: 01604 858372. Village 'local' offering bar and restaurant food. Hook Norton etc. Pool, darts and skittles. NN7 3BU

Shopping

General store and post office in main street of village.

Connections

BUSES - services 88/9 to/from Northampton, Towcester and Milton Keynes; every 30 minutes Mon-Sat, every 90 minutes Suns. Tel: 0871 200 2233.

Stoke Bruerne   Map 20

Stoke Bruerne transcends its popularity. In high season it attracts the sort of ice cream crowds which many a theme park would envy. Yet it contrives to retain its integrity, remaining a tight-knit community with a mildly obsessive interest in the welfare of its canal. Trip boats offer land borne visitors the chance to briefly get afloat, and three gift shops offer no alibi for returning home empty-handed.

Eating & Drinking

THE BOAT INN - canalside above top lock. Tel: 01604 862428. Thatched 'local' popular with visitors and villagers alike which has been run by the same family since 1877. Regular *Good Beer Guide* entry.

Northamptonshire skittles. Restaurant with view over canal to mill and museum. Bistro, breakfasts, basic provisions. NN12 7SB

SPICE OF BRUERNE - canalside Indian restaurant, also offering take-away service and free delivery within 4 miles radius. Tel: 01604 863654 - NN12 7SB

THE NAVIGATION - Bridge 53. Tel: 01604 864988. Marston's all-day pub with canal-themed interior. Open from 10am. Waterside tables. NN12 7SY

Things to Do

THE CANAL MUSEUM - Tel: 01604 862229. Open daily 10am to 5pm in Summer. Closed Mon & Tue in Winter. Cafe. Admission charge. Charming collection of authentic and well-displayed artefacts. NN12 7SE

Connections

BUSES - Stagecoach service 86 offers four Mon-Sat journeys to/from Towcester and/or Northampton. The bus stop is by Bridge 53. Tel: 0871 200 2233.

21 GRAND UNION CANAL Stoke Locks 4.5mls/5lks/3hrs

NORTHAMPTONSHIRE is a county more travelled through than visited. Lines of communication stretch across its hedged fields like strings across the frets on the neck of a guitar.

Perhaps that explains why these roads and railways, and this canal, appear aloof from the landscape. "Sorry, can't stop," they seem to be saying: "We're just passing through."

The canal traveller spends two hours negotiating the six mile pound between Stoke Bruerne and Cosgrove: a lonely landscape characterised by ridge & furrow pasturelands. Besides a diverting succession of wide spill-weirs, the only major landmarks are the manor house and church on the brow of the hill at Grafton, the wharf and mooring lagoon at Yardley (where you are warned to beware 'elderly ducks'), and the lofty, flying-buttressed spire of Hanslope church to the east.

Few outside the county of Northamptonshire will claim to know the course of the River Tove, but by the time it joins the Great Ouse at

Cosgrove it is a significant watercourse. It rises on the uplands east of Banbury, not far from Sulgrave Manor. At the foot of Stoke locks one arm of the river - used for private moorings - flows into the canal, whilst the other passes beneath the man-made waterway. The Tove forms the boundary with Buckinghamshire, a county of considerable length. Olney seems a long way from Dorney.

Stoke Locks form another step in the Grand Union's roller-coaster ride between London and Birmingham: the old Grand Junction Canal had summits at Tring and Braunston; when the route was amalgamated with the Warwick & Birmingham Canal in 1929, a third summit was added at Olton, near Solihull. A pump house, dated 1939, returns water from the foot of the flight to the top, but another water saving economy, the use of side ponds, is no longer in use. Subjectively, the canal seems quieter. Can it be that many boaters hardly go beyond Yardley Gobion?

Between the foot of Stoke Locks and Thrupp Wharf (Map 22) the towpath is narrow and bumpy. Both walkers and cyclists will get through but not without the odd imprecation or two.

spw = spill-weir

BOUNDARIES fluctuate at the best of times; be they personal, political, or merely perceived. In the Grand Union's crossing of the Great Ouse at Cosgrove you could argue that you are passing from the midlands to the south, from a region historically associated with billowing chimneys, to one of bucolic charm ... but then you bump into the old railway workshops of Wolverton, and all those comfortably accumulated preconceptions are abruptly and rudely contradicted. And if we have trouble, emotionally, crossing the Great Ouse, spare a thought for Jessop and the canal builders who had to solve it physically. It would be a wastage of time and water to lock down and up again, so they aspired to an aqueduct. But that in itself would take time to build, and time was money, so they built a temporary flight of locks either side whilst a masonry aqueduct of three arches was being constructed on dry land, the intention being to divert the river beneath it upon completion. The locks were in use by 1802, four to the south and five to the north. Lock 21 is the only one which remains, hinting at the original alignment. One of the chambers on the opposite (southern) bank has been cosmetically restored along with succinct inter-pretive panels. Canal historians ponder the practicalities of horse-drawn boats negotiating the occasionally fast flowing river. Was some sort of timber walkway provided, and if so, on which side? The past has as many possibilities as the future, that's why we love it so. In the event Jessop's aqueduct didn't last long. It collapsed in 1808, forcing the denizens of Stony Stratford to go around in wellingtons for a week*. In the three years which

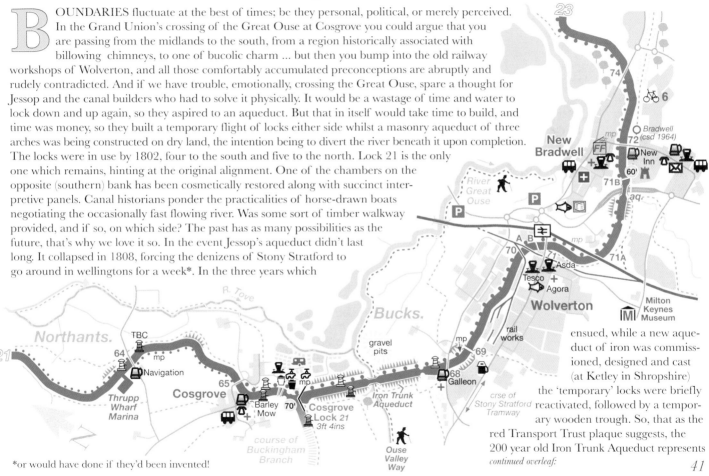

ensued, while a new aque-duct of iron was commiss-ioned, designed and cast (at Ketley in Shropshire) the 'temporary' locks were briefly reactivated, followed by a tempor-ary wooden trough. So, that as the red Transport Trust plaque suggests, the 200 year old Iron Trunk Aqueduct represents

*or would have done if they'd been invented!

continued overleaf:

continued from page 41:

the fourth attempt to cross the valley. Note how the towpath, contrary to Pontcysyllte, is cantilevered out from the iron trunk. A path at the southern end leads down to the riverbank, and you can squeeze through a 'cattle creep' to view the aqueduct from the opposite side.

Immediately above Cosgrove Lock, a short arm used for private moorings, is, in fact, the route of the former Old Stratford & Buckingham branch which measured ten miles and featured two locks. A pretty, but not conspicuously viable canal, the most interesting facet of its operation was the establishment of a boatbuilding yard, away from the canal itself, at Stony Stratford, specialising in the construction of small sea-going vessels which had to be hauled by traction engine along the Watling Street and launched into the canal for transfer to London. The Bucking-

ham Canal Society are actively pursuing restoration.

Wolverton isn't as well known as it used to be for its railway works, but it continues to be home to the Royal Train. The workshops specialised in the manufacture and maintenance of carriages, and at their height employed the best part of five thousand people. Two intrinsically different railways brought them to work: the Stony Stratford Tramway, a 3ft 6ins gauge street running line of double-decker cars hauled by little skirted steam engines not unlike *Thomas the Tank Engine's* chum *Toby* in appearance; and the Newport Pagnell branch, which was laid on the bed of an earlier canal - see Map 23. The tramway closed in 1926, in the wake of the General Strike, the staff simply never returned. The last 'Newport Nobby' puffed by in 1964, an unsung casualty of the Beeching Report.

Cosgrove
Map 22

A quiet village away from the main road with some attractive stone buildings. An unusual pedestrian tunnel (once used by boat horses to reach the pub stables) passes beneath the canal, whilst, for reasons never satisfactorily explained, Bridge 65 is unusually ornate. A narrow gauge railway linked sand pits in the valley with the canal wharf and some of the rails remain in situ by the old canal junction.

Eating & Drinking
THE NAVIGATION - Thrupp Wharf (Bridge 64). Tel: 01908 543156. Greene King beers, bar/restaurant food. MK19 7BE
BARLEY MOW - The Stocks (offside south of Bridge 65). Tel: 01908 562957. Customer moorings. Everards beers. Food, Northampton skittles. MK19 7JD

Shopping
Groceries obtainable from the caravan park stores adjacent to Cosgrove Lock.

Connections
BUSES - service 90 to/from Northampton and Milton Keynes - Tel: 0871 200 2233.

Wolverton
Map 22

A slice of Crewe in rural Buckinghamshire.

Eating & Drinking
THE GALLEON - adjacent to Bridge 68 where the canal widens and there are good moorings. Tel: 01908 321711. MK12 5NL
BUSKERS - The Triangle (access via Bridge 70B). Tel: 01908 310165. Award-winning coffee shop/sandwich bar delightfully housed in music shop. Open from 8am (8.30am Suns) to 5.30pm (4pm Suns) plus selected Supper Evenings. MK12 5FJ

Shopping
Tesco and Asda supermarkets easily reached from Bridge 70B. Agora indoor market and charity bookshop housed in former LNWR Fire Station premises.

Things to Do
MILTON KEYNES MUSEUM - McConnell Drive. Tel: 01908 316222. Homely little museum devoted to the area's past featuring (amongst much else) a section devoted to McCorquodales and a restored Stony

Connections
TRAINS - frequent London Midland services from canalside station to/from Northampton, Milton Keynes Leighton Buzzard etc. Tel: 08457 484950.

New Bradwell
Map 22

A community of terraced streets built as homes for the employees of Wolverton railway works.

Eating & Drinking
THE NEW INN - Tel: 01908 310155. Charles Wells canalside pub offering a wide range of food commencing with breakfasts from 10am. MK13 0EW.
NAPOLI - the wonderful fish & chip shop on Newport Road, owned by second generation Italian, Luciano Pilla - Tel: 01908 313193.

Shopping
Co-op with cash machine less than 5 minutes walk from Bridge 72.

Things to Do
BRADWELL MILL - see Milton Keynes Museum, Wolverton. The windmill is open selected Sundays and Bank Holidays.

Map labels:

- Monks Way
- M1
- N
- Pagoda
- Portway
- Childs Way
- Woolstone
- Woughton
- Barge Inn
- mp
- Olde Swan
- P
- P
- Willen Park
- Gullivers
- 81B
- M
- 6
- Springfield
- Brickhill Street
- Downhead Park
- 81
- 80A
- 81A
- 82
- 70'
- 82A/B
- 83
- 84
- 85
- 85A
- 86
- 87
- 88
- mp
- 89
- 6
- 79C
- 79D
- Campbell Park
- MILTON KEYNES
- Marlborough Street
- Milton Keynes Marina
- 24
- mp
- 79B
- Pennyland
- 79A
- Giffard Park
- Gt Linford (csd - 1964)
- FF
- 78B
- 79
- LCC
- 78
- 78A
- mp
- 77
- 70'
- P
- Great Linford
- Nags Head
- Black Horse
- 76
- 76A
- P
- 6
- mp
- 75
- 22

THE future is a foreign country: they do things differently there. In the hope that L. P. Hartley won't spin in his grave at our purloining and inversion of the sentence which so oft'-quotedly opens *The Go-Between*, Milton Keynes Development Corporation's forward-looking template of the 1970s has resulted in a sprawling city of quarter of a million souls that bears little resemblance to the Britain most of us know, and if not love, at least feel comfortable in. Few would take issue with the scheme's journey from drawing-board to reality - it appears to have achieved everything it set so boldly out to do - but if you leave the canal for a moment and take to the winding, lamplit and largely litter-free footpaths, a certain unease bubbles to the surface: is this an immaculate conception with overtones of Scandinavian noir?

Oh yes, the *canal*! Well, it's easy to overlook that it predates the city by a century and a half. Old maps show it traversing a rolling landscape of scattered hamlets, and the working boatmen of the past would surely be nonplussed at the transformation. The only canalside settlements of any note along this section were at Great Linford and Woughton-on-the-Green. The former was notable as the point - just east of Bridge 77 - from which a branch canal led to Newport Pagnell. It had been opened in 1817 but was closed by 1846, much of its course being taken over by the railway alluded to on Map 22, itself now converted into a pleasant public footpath and cycleway. The prominent canalside building was formerly a pub called the Old Wharf. And, incidentally, a side-street just over the bridge on the towpath side was given the name Willow Wren in homage to the carrying company. A nice touch, typical of MK's considerate respect for the past it obliterated.

Boaters and walkers will take a couple of hours to work their way through this Brave New World of 21st century living. Cyclists may find the poplar-lined Canal Broadway a more conducive surface than the sometimes narrow towpath. How do *you* respond? The variety of architectural
continued overleaf:

for details of facilities throughout Milton Keynes turn to page 44

continued from page 43:

styles is as diverse as it is eclectic. One welcomes the good honest use of brick and timber, the refusal to be hidebound and categorised; the informality, the heterogeneity, the vernacular splashes of weatherboarding and pantiles; the canal's role as a linear park. But what comes as a surprise is the sheer un-Englishness of it all: communal drives, patios and lawns seem at odds with native Anglo-Saxon reserve, as though Milton Keynes was the blueprint for a new generation of gregarious Britons, brought up on ('Come on Down') *The Price is Right.*

The Bedford & Milton Keynes Waterway Trust was formed in 1995 to promote a brand new, sixteen mile, broad beam link between Great Ouse at Kempston and the Grand Union Canal at Bridge 82A. An exciting project, by any stretch of the imagination, it would provide a ground-breaking link with the inland waterways of eastern England. Technically it is do-able. But whether or not funding in the region of £40 million can be sourced in these straitened times is another matter.

Milton Keynes Map 23

The canal system throws up many paradoxes - some humorous, some delightful, some patently absurd - and the fact that the Canal & River Trust, guardians of our waterway heritage, have their headquarters in a faceless modern office block overlooking the railway station in this most futuristically hi-tech of cities is just about as ludicrous as you can get.

Eating & Drinking

BLACK HORSE - Wolverton Road, Great Linford (adjacent Bridge 76). Tel: 01908 398461. Pleasantly refurbished canalside pub. MK14 5AJ

NAGS HEAD - High Street, Great Linford (access from offside visitor moorings between bridges 76A and 77. Tel: 01908 607449. Whitewashed/thatched 15th century pub. MK14 5AX

GIFFARD PARK - Giffard Park (adjacent visitor moorings west of Bridge 78). Tel: 01908 210025. Sizzling Pubs restaurant/bar. MK14 5QN

CAMPHILL CAFE - Japonica Lane (adjacent Bridge 81). Tel: 01908 235000. Nice little vegetarian cafe staffed by adults with learning difficulties, open 10.30am-4.30pm Mon-Fri. Shop with freshly baked bread, home-grown fruit and veg. MK15 9JY

BARGE INN - Newport Road, Woolstone (access from bridges 83/4). Tel: 01908 233841. Vintage Inns group pub. MK15 0AE

Peace Pagoda

PEARTREE BRIDGE INN - canalside Bridge 88. Tel: 01908 691515. Crown Carvery restaurant/pub at MK Marina. MK6 3PE

YE OLDE SWAN - Newport Road, Woughton (east of Bridge 88). Tel: 01908 679489. Quaint Chef & Brewer pub. MK6 3BS

Shopping

The main shopping area lies about one and a half miles west of the canal: 'half a mile of covered shopping' they boast; a salutary reminder of why you escaped onto the canals in the first place. The modestly-stocked post office stores at Giffard Park is the *only* provisions outlet beside the canal.

Things to Do

PEACE PAGODA - 6 minutes walk from Bridge 81. A thousand specially planted cherry and cedar trees enshrine the memory of victims of all war, whilst the pagoda itself, erected in 1980 by the nuns and monks of Nipponzan Myohoji - stands in the specific hope that the earth will be spared from nuclear annihilation. So far so good ...

BLETCHLEY PARK - Sherwood Drive, Bletchley (300 yards from Bletchley railway station - accessible by bus from MK or train from Fenny Stratford (Map 24). Tel: 01908 640404. The celebrated home of code breaking in World War II. MK3 6EB

GULLIVERS LAND - Newlands. (adjacent Bridge 81B and Campbell Park visitor moorings. Tel: 01908 609001. Children's theme park ages 2-13. MK15 0DT

Connections

BUSES - regular/frequent services operate from the canalside settlements of Great Linford (24/5), Gifford Park (2), Woolstone/Woughton (18) to/from central Milton Keynes and its railway station. Ditto along Portway (40, 300, X5), Childs Way (8 etc) and Marlborough Street (4 etc). Tel: 0871 200 2233. TRAINS - Virgin and London Midland services from station in Central MK. Tel: 08457 484950. TAXIS - ACE. Tel: 01908 555555.

FENNY STRATFORD Lock marks the commencement of the Grand Union's climb out of the valley of the Ouse up towards the Chilterns and the summit at Tring. But, with a rise of a meagre foot, its contribution to the ascent is not impressive. In fact, it was not planned in the original survey, being built as a supposedly temporary measure to alleviate excess water pressures experienced on the long pound between here and Cosgrove. Tradition has it that southbound working boats in a hurry used to burst their way through whichever gates happened to be shut at the time, a habit the authorities would doubtless respond to with court summonses today. In any case, the lock (straddled by a swing-bridge in a manner reminiscent of Hungerford) comes as welcome exercise after the three or four hours spent glued to the tiller if you have come straight down from Cosgrove.

'Finney' marks the southern extent of Milton Keynes' sprawl. Travelling southwards it is, in many ways, reassuring to be back in the familiar world of semi-detached suburbs. Fenny Wharf was a busy spot: coal was brought to the gas works and flour and sugar carried from London Docks to Valentine's mill. The railway - truncated post-Beeching - used to link the university cities of Oxford and Cambridge. The little station exudes considerable half-timbered charm.

As the canal emerges from its urban environment there are pleasant views across the River Ouzel and Watling Street towards the elevated heathlands of Woburn and Aspley. Northwards from Fenny Stratford the Grand Union is bordered briefly by factories before skirting the old village of Simpson on an embankment. A small aqueduct, invisible from the waterline, accommodates a footpath. There are glimpses to the east of Walton Hall, headquarters of the Open University.

Summary of Facilities

The Plough Inn (Tel: 01908 691555 - MK6 3AH) at Simpson is handily canalside and mooring is feasible if informal. With Italian hosts, the emphasis is, unsurprisingly, on that country's cooking. The beers are from slightly closer to home, Charles Wells of Bedford. Bus 18 runs to/from Milton Keynes.

The Red Lion (Tel: 01908 372317 - MK1 1BY) at Fenny Stratford is a *Good Beer Guide* regular, not somewhere to eat, but to sup well-kept beer and watch rookie boat crews fathom out the swing-bridge over the lock. 'Finney' seems more and more bereft of shops each time we pass, notwithstanding Pollard's marvellous ironmongery. If you're desperate, there's a large Tesco 15 minutes walk along Watling Street north-west of Bridge 96 or an M&S convenience store at the petrol station on Aylesbury Street. There are two Indian restaurants/take-aways, a Chinese, and an excellent fish & chip shop. Trains run hourly (Mon-Sat) to Bletchley (for main line connections) and Bedford.

25 GRAND UNION CANAL Stoke Hammond 5mls/4lks/2.5hrs

THE Grand Union has probably appeared more often in canal literature than any other waterway. Classics, fictional and factual, like *The Water Gipsies*, *Maiden's Trip*, *Voyage in a Bowler Hat*, *Hold on a Minute*, and *Bread Upon the Waters*, successfully capture its atmosphere as a working waterway, but don't really prepare you for its beauty as it unravels through the Ouzel Valley, past the sandy, bracken covered hills of Linslade and over the border from Bucks to Beds. The Ouzel seems to shift some of its riverine quality upon the canal; as in all good friendships, there is a degree of exchange in character. The river rises on Dunstable Downs and flows northwards to join the Great Ouse at Newport Pagnell. It used to be a river of many watermills, some of which survive very prettily as private dwellings.

Stoke Hammond is one of Britain's 'Thankful Villages'; fifty-one out of sixteen thousand whose First World War servicemen all returned safely home. Soulbury Locks - known to working boatmen as the 'Stoke Hammond Three' (which sounds more like an organ-based jazz combo appearing in some smoky Soho dive

circa 1956) - are often graced by a volunteer lock-keeper nowadays. The three mile pound between Soulbury and Leighton locks is captivating. Beyond the watermeadows of the Ouzel, mixed woodland clothes a ridge of heathland. Swing-bridge 112 recedes into the undergrowth a bit more each time we pass; the unenviable fate of old swingers everywhere.

Summary of Facilities

Two well known canalside pubs tempt you to pause along this length of canal. At Soulbury Locks the Three Locks (Tel: 01525 270214 - MK17 9DD) does a roaring trade with motorists fascinated by the activity of the locks. A wide range of meals are served and the pub is open from noon daily. Of equal popularity, The Globe (Tel: 01525 373338 - LU7 2TA) by Bridge 111 is a much older building, attractively weatherboarded outside and beamed within. It belongs to Greene King's 'Old English Inns' group. Stoke Hammond's stores are open from 6am (7am Suns) through to 10pm daily. Arriva bus service 70 links Stoke Hammond and Soulbury Locks with Milton Keynes and Leighton Buzzard, hourly Mon-Sat. Tel: 0871 200 2233.

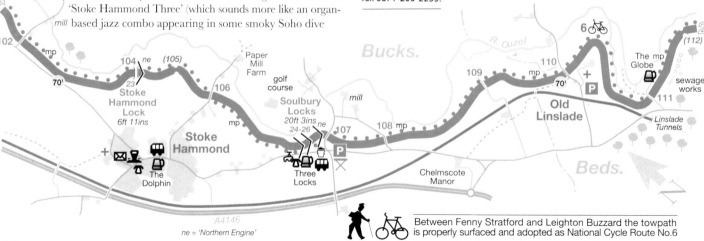

Between Fenny Stratford and Leighton Buzzard the towpath is properly surfaced and adopted as National Cycle Route No.6

INTERRUPTED briefly - but not overwhelmed - by the shared urban environments of Linslade and Leighton Buzzard, the Grand Union Canal continues its predominantly rural progress, crossing the boundary between the counties of Bedford and Buckingham. Solitary locks come along at regular intervals, each with its own atmosphere and ambience. Leighton Lock is overlooked by a substantial, whitewashed lock-keeper's house; near Grove Lock there is a stone milepost advertising the distance to the Thames; and adjacent to Church Lock what was once the smallest chapel in Buckinghamshire has been converted into a private residence.

In the early years of the Grand Junction water shortages were experienced and, to go some way to alleviate the problem, a sequence of narrowbeam chambers were duplicated alongside the original wide locks. These permitted single boats to use less water, and also enabled the canal to cope better with its growing traffic. Remains of these locks are apparent at several locations and explain the provision of extra arches on a number of bridges. A series of pumping engines was also introduced to return water to the summit. Most of the characteristic engine houses remain. Working boatmen called them the 'Northern Engines', and naturally there were regular deliveries of coal by boat to stoke the boilers. Another local cargo was sand and there is plenty of evidence of former wharves, one still with track embedded in the towpath where narrow gauge railways ran to connect such loading points with the sand pits themselves. The Linslade-based carrying fleet of L. B. Faulkner - which at its zenith in the 1920s consisted of nearly fifty boats - also dealt with this traffic, notably with regular deliveries to the Chance Brothers glassworks at Smethwick.

Leighton Buzzard has its place in the early annals of aviation history. At Morgan's canalside engineering works, the First World War Vickers Vimy bomber was developed at a site now occupied by Tesco who pay homage to posterity with an appropriately shaped weathervane. The 'Dunstable Dasher' last puffed across Bridge 115A on 30th June 1962.

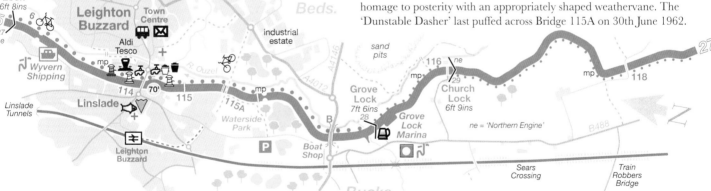

for details of facilities at Leighton Buzzard turn to page 48

Leighton Buzzard
Map 26

Lured in by the two hundred foot high spire of All Saints, you'll find LB an unexpectedly delightful town (as opposed to LA) with a refreshing period feel; especially on Tuesdays and Saturdays when the handsome High Street throbs with the activity of an excellent street market. A wealth of solid, provincial architecture spans the centuries - a perfect antidote to the high-tech of MK, elevating Leighton into arguably the most amenable town on the old Grand Junction north of Berkhamsted.

Eating & Drinking

GROVE LOCK - canalside Lock 28. Tel: 01525 380940. Comfortable Fullers pub (a harbinger of London!) serving food from noon daily. LU7 0QU
GOLDEN BELL - Church Square. Tel: 01525 373330. *Good Beer Guide* listed town pub. LU7 1AE
SWAN HOTEL - High Street. Tel: 01525 380170. Imposing *GBG* listed town centre hotel renovated by Wetherspoons, and offering, along with inexpensive food and accommodation, their usual wide range of real ales. LU7 1EA
PIZZA EXPRESS - Market Square. Tel: 01525 384560. Pizza and pasta staple housed in pretty little clock-towered Fire Station of 1919. LU7 1EU

Shopping

Some distinctive local shops in the town centre, notably the butcher H. G. Stratton (est. 1936) on Market Square. Farmers market 3rd Sat; Handmade market 4th. Canalside Tesco (with recycling point), nearby Aldi, town centre Waitrose and Morrisons. Puncture repairs at Dorvic's on Bridge Street!

Things to Do

LEIGHTON BUZZARD RAILWAY - Billington Road. Tel: 01525 373888. Charming narrow-gauge railway based on former sand-carrying system. LU7 4TN

Connections

TRAINS - frequent London Midland services along the Northampton-Milton Keynes-Berkhamsted corridor. Tel: 08457 484950.
BUSES - Arriva service 70 runs hourly (Mon-Sat) northwards via Stoke Hammond to Milton Keynes, and eastwards half-hourly (bi-hourly Suns) to Dunstable and Luton. Tel: 0871 200 2233.
TAXIS - 3A's. Tel: 01525 851000.

Slapton
Map 27

CARPENTER'S ARMS - Horton Road (half a mile NE of Br. 120). Tel: 01525 220563. 16th century pub of thatch and brick. Bar and restaurant food, locally sourced real ales. LU7 9DB

Cheddington
Map 27

Straggling commuter village, noted for its ancient cultivation terraces, or 'lynchets'.

Eating & Drinking

OLD SWAN - High Street. Tel: 01296 668226. Artisan bistro & bar best reached from Bridge 126. Open from 11am daily. LU7 0RQ
THREE HORSESHOES - Mentmore Street. Tel: 01296 668367. Homely village local open from noon daily. Meals at lunchtimes, and evenings (ex Sat & Sun). LU7 0SD

Shopping

Convenience store deep in a housing estate.

Connections

TRAINS - isolated station (from which there are views of Mentmore, once the country seat of the Rothschilds) served by London Midland trains between MK and Euston, forming a useful staging post between Leighton Buzzard and Tring for the benefit of towpath walkers. Tel: 08457 484950.
TAXIS - Cheddington Taxis. Tel: 01296 661666.

Ivinghoe
Map 27

Picturesque village which was once a small market town at the bifurcation of the Icknield Ways. Walks to the panoramic summit of the beacon.

Eating & Drinking

KINGS HEAD - Station Road. Tel: 01296 668388. Fine dining in ivy-clad building dating from the 16th century. Famed for its Aylesbury Duck! LU7 9EB
ROSE & CROWN - Vicarage Lane. Award-winning community pub. Open from 11am daily (5pm Mons). Tel: 01296 668472. LU7 9EQ
HALDI - Marsworth Road. Tel: 01296 662204. Indian restaurant/take-away. LU7 9AS

Shopping

Convenience store & post office housed in former Town Hall.

Things to Do

PITSTONE WINDMILL - Tel: 01442 851227. Lovely timber post mill cared for by the National Trust. you can view it at any time, but it's open to the public on Sunday afternoons June-August.
FORD END WATERMILL - Station Road. Tel: 01442 825421. Ancient watermill dating from the middle ages and in commercial use up until 1963. Open selected Sunday and Bank Holiday afternoons and milling when water levels permit. LU7 9EA
PITSTONE GREEN MUSEUM - Vicarage Road. Tel: 01582 605464. Category-defying museum, ostensibly of rural life, though much else besides: aviation and militaria, industrial archaeology, model railways et al. Open selected Sundays and Bank holidays 11am-5pm. Refreshments. LU7 9EY

Connections

BUSES - Arriva service 61 to/from Aylesbury & Dunstable. Sunday bus 50 links Ivinghoe with Tring, Wendover and Aylesbury. Tel: 0871 200 2233.

SAND gives way to clay, and clay to chalk, as the canal begins to take seriously the responsibility of climbing up to The Chilterns. Locks occur more frequently, and there is little point in those responsible for working them reboarding the boat in the intervening pounds. In any case it's fun to tramp along the reasonably well-maintained towpath for a change, gazing eastwards to the furzy escarpment of the Dunstable Downs where, when the light is right, you can clearly discern the chalk lion of Whipsnade (cut in 1933 as an advertisement for the nascent zoo) and watch gliders making the most of upwardly mobile thermals above the rounded rampart of Ivinghoe Beacon, 757ft above sea level.

A sense of remoteness casts a spell over the countryside. The boat people knew this stretch of canal as "The Fields", a typically simple yet eloquent description. This isolation is underlined when you recall that the Great Train Robbery took place on the lonely section of line north of Cheddington station on 8th August 1963. The southbound Travelling Post Office, Glasgow-London mail was hijacked at Sears Crossing and relieved of its £2.6 million* booty at Bridego Bridge (Map 26); now known as Train Robbers Bridge. The long railway embankment was built from Tring Cutting's spoil. Luton Angling Club's elongated and zealously signposted piscatorial beat seems to last indefinitely.

The Grand Junction was a canal obsessed with time. Everything was date-stamped: lock chambers, bridges, tie bars, mooring rings, paddle gear. You are tempted to indulge in a sort of Victorian parlour game in which you must attach an important event to each date you come across. Boating is brisk by Cooks Wharf where the Dunstable & District Boat Club have extensive moorings. Round the corner, tucked in between the road and railway bridges, is Grebe Canal Cruises' busy boatyard which boasts its own waterside cafe.

B489 to Dunstable
B488 to Tring

Ivinghoe

Pitstone Windmill (NT)

Pitstone Museum

Pitstone

Ford End Watermill

Ivinghoe Beacon

34
123
122
35
36
125
mp
ne
ne
33
126
Cooks Wharf
DDBC
Cultivation Terraces

Whipsnade Lion

Horton Wharf

121
ne 31
mp 32

ne = 'Northern Engine'

Old Swan

Cheddington

Carpenters Arms

Slapton

70'
120
mp 50
30
ne

Three H'shoes

Mentmore

crse of Aylesbury Railway

26

Locks
30 Slapton Lock 7ft 0ins
31 Horton Lock 6ft 9ins
32 & 33 Ivinghoe Locks 14ft 3ins
34-36 Seabrook Locks 20ft 4ins

* You can comfortably multiply that twentyfold now.

28 GRAND UNION CANAL Marsworth & Tring 3mls/9lks/3hrs*

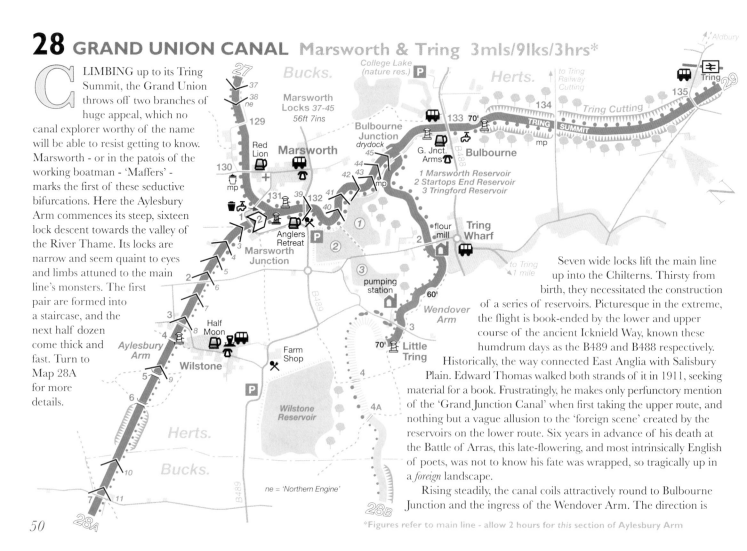

CLIMBING up to its Tring Summit, the Grand Union throws off two branches of huge appeal, which no canal explorer worthy of the name will be able to resist getting to know. Marsworth - or in the patois of the working boatman - 'Maffers' - marks the first of these seductive bifurcations. Here the Aylesbury Arm commences its steep, sixteen lock descent towards the valley of the River Thame. Its locks are narrow and seem quaint to eyes and limbs attuned to the main line's monsters. The first pair are formed into a staircase, and the next half dozen come thick and fast. Turn to Map 28A for more details.

Seven wide locks lift the main line up into the Chilterns. Thirsty from birth, they necessitated the construction of a series of reservoirs. Picturesque in the extreme, the flight is book-ended by the lower and upper course of the ancient Icknield Way, known these humdrum days as the B489 and B488 respectively. Historically, the way connected East Anglia with Salisbury Plain. Edward Thomas walked both strands of it in 1911, seeking material for a book. Frustratingly, he makes only perfunctory mention of the 'Grand Junction Canal' when first taking the upper route, and nothing but a vague allusion to the 'foreign scene' created by the reservoirs on the lower route. Six years in advance of his death at the Battle of Arras, this late-flowering, and most intrinsically English of poets, was not to know his fate was wrapped, so tragically up in a *foreign* landscape.

Rising steadily, the canal coils attractively round to Bulbourne Junction and the ingress of the Wendover Arm. The direction is

Map labels:
- 27
- Bucks.
- College Lake (nature res.)
- to Tring Railway Cutting
- Herts.
- Tring
- 29
- Aldbury
- 37
- 38
- ne
- 129
- Marsworth Locks 37-45 56ft 7ins
- 134
- Tring Cutting
- TRING SUMMIT
- 135
- Red Lion
- Marsworth
- Bulbourne Junction
- drydock
- 45
- 133
- 70'
- G. Jnct. Arms
- Bulbourne
- 130
- mp
- 44
- 43
- 42
- mp
- 1 Marsworth Reservoir
- 2 Startops End Reservoir
- 3 Tringford Reservoir
- 131
- 39
- 132
- 41
- 40
- 1
- 2
- Anglers Retreat
- Marsworth Junction
- 3
- flour mill
- Tring Wharf
- to Tring 1 mile
- pumping station
- 60'
- Wendover Arm
- 3
- 4
- 5
- 6
- 7
- Half Moon
- 8
- Aylesbury Arm
- Wilstone
- 4
- 5
- 9
- Farm Shop
- 70'
- Little Tring
- 4
- 4A
- 6
- Wilstone Reservoir
- Herts.
- Bucks.
- 10
- 7
- 11
- 28A
- ne = 'Northern Engine'
- B489
- 28B

*Figures refer to main line - allow 2 hours for *this* section of Aylesbury Arm deliberately implied, for the arm was built to supply water to the main line from springs and artesian wells in the Chiltern Hills. Opened in 1797, the Wendover Arm was constructed to the same broad gauge dimensions as the main line and a fair amount of trade developed. Furthermore the notable boatbuilding yard of Bushell Bros, was established at Tring Wharf. But ironically - given its primary use as a supply channel - the arm's central section was prone to leakage and had to be dewatered in 1904, a pipe being laid beneath the canal bed to guarantee continued water supply.

The Wendover Arm might thus have been consigned to history as just another 'lost canal' but for its championing by the Wendover Arm Trust who are gradually restoring it to navigation. Currently boats can travel as far as Little Tring where, in idyllic, swift-haunted surroundings, 48 hour visitor moorings are provided together with a full length winding-hole. The arm is shallow and progress by boat slow, but explorers are not by nature hurriers and, in the fullness of canal time, the first overbridge appears and, immediately beyond it, a large and flourishing flour mill. It was here, where Heygates park their lorries now, that Bushells had their boatyard. Tringford pumping station dates from 1818 and continues to fulfil - along with the neighbouring resevoirs - an important role in providing the Grand Union Canal with water, though the original Boulton & Watt steam engines were replaced by diesel-electric pumps in 1911. A stop lock once stood alongside the pumping station. Bridge 3 was rebuilt in 2005, the original had been demolished in the 1970s. A few hundred yards further on the arm reaches it present terminus, a plaque recording the part a legacy from Tim (*Hold*

on a Minute - see also page 59) Wilkinson played in reaching thus far.

The ensuing, 'dry' section of the canal between Little Tring and Drayton Beauchamp (Map 28B) is the one which suffered leakage problems almost from the outset. WCT have been painstakingly working to re-open this length and render it watertight for the first time in its history, work which will enable navigation to be returned as far as the winding hole between bridges 5A and 5B in the forseeable future. In the meantime, walkers can proceed comfortably all the way from Little Tring to Wendover (Map 28B) albeit with a slight detour at the outset.

Focusing, once again, on the main line, the environs of Bulbourne Junction itself repay investigation, consisting, as they do, of a covered drydock, a reedy side-pond, a substantial junction house, and the elegant Bulbourne workshops where lock gate manufacture took place until 2004. However British Waterways abandoned the site and it is now occupied by a firm specialising in ornamental ironwork who have a gallery open to the public. Beyond the depot the canal passes beneath the Upper Icknield Way and enters Tring Cutting. Stretching for one and a half miles, and reaching a maximum depth of thirty feet, the cutting is said to have taken the best part of five years to dig. With equipment no more sophisticated than pick-axes and wheel-barrows, this is hardly surprising. But the labour of two centuries ago seems nebulous now. Nature long ago reclaimed the gash in her side, soothed it with vegetation, and created a chasm of narcotic splendour. By way of contrast, a short walk north-east of Bridge 134 reveals Robert Stephenson's railway equivalent of 1838.

Marsworth
Map 28

An unassuming, shopless village on the border of Bucks and Herts, dominated by a flint-towered church.

Eating & Drinking
RED LION - adjacent Bridge 130. Tel: 01296 668366. *Good Beer Guide* listed village pub long favoured by canal travellers. Comfortable sofas, comforting food and conversation, comforting local ales. Perennially one of the nicest pubs of the GU! HP23 4LU

ANGLERS RETREAT - adjacent Bridge 132. Tel: 01442 822250. Pub grub, Tring Brewery beers and bed & breakfast. HP23 4LJ
BLUEBELL'S - Lock 39. Tel: 01442 891708. Tearooms handy for the locks and the reservoirs. HP23 4LJ

Connections
BUSES - Red Line service 164 runs, thrice daily, Mon-Sat between Aylesbury and Leighton Buzzard. Tel: 0871 200 2233.

Wilstone
Map 28

Small village alongside the Aylesbury Arm. Little pub called the Half Moon (Tel: 01442 826410 - HP23 4PD), community shop (7.30am-2pm Mon-Fri (1pm Sat; 9am-12pm Sun), and farm shop with tea room.

Bulbourne
Map 28

No shops, but the Grand Junction Arms (Tel: 01442 891400 - HP23 5QE) by Bridge 133 is a popular pub.

Pitstone Mill

Bulbourne

Leighton Buzzard

Braunston Tunnel

Marsworth

GREENOCK

Echoes
from the Shires

Cosgrove

Blisworth

52

Gasworks & Cemetery

Slough Arm

Kings Langley Poplars

Frogmore Papermill

Kensal Town

Bridgewater Monument, Ashridge

London Calling

53

THE Aylesbury Arm has experienced its fair share of vicissitudes in recent times, there have been infrastructure failures and its far end is in the throes of redevelopment, and the Aylesbury Canal Society - who have presided like genial hosts over the terminal basin for years - have decamped to a new site on the edge of town. Nevertheless, we have always had a soft spot for this lovely branch canal, which spills down into the Vale like an apple-cart rumbling along a country lane. For a couple of miles the arm passes into Hertfordshire, but the landscape remains aloof, the inherent peace of the canal being broken only by the inane hooting of car horns as they approach each hump-backed bridge. But at this point you will probably be impatient for facts, even though, as Sir John Squire once ruefully pointed out, they are only flies in the amber. The bare essentials are that the canal was promoted late in the 18th century as a through route across the Vale of Aylesbury to the Thames at Abingdon, from whence connection would be made via the Wilts & Berks and Kennet & Avon canals to Bath and Bristol. What a mouth-watering canal odyssey that would have made possible. In the event, only the arm to Aylesbury materialised and, following its opening in 1815, it settled down to a century and a half of trade, notably the carrying activities of the well known boat company Harvey-Taylor whose motor *Roger* is preserved at Rickmansworth (Map 33).

Although the Aylesbury Arm is essentially a rural canal there is much to draw the alert eye. As you proceed across the border into Herts (Map 28) there are views to the north of Mentmore, designed by Paxton for one of the Rothschilds. Soon the flint tower of Marsworth church is left astern and, as the gradient eases, the locks come less closely spaced. Lock 9 is sweetly called 'Gudgeon Stream'. A huge new dairy has been built alongside the canal between bridges 8 and 9. Red House Lock is named after an isolated inn of the same name which stood alongside it, but which was converted into a private residence in the mid Sixties. Beyond here the channel narrows perceptibly and tall reeds seem to whisper like rumourmongers as you pass. From the perspective of the towpath it feels as if this is not a canalside walk at all, but rather a route-march through a maize field. Indeed, one expects to encounter a fleeing Cary Grant at any moment. Herons are numerous, as are human fishermen. Closely related species, the easiest way to tell them apart is that herons are said to smile occasionally. When we first became acquainted with the arm, in the 1980s, industry jostled its banks, the nearer Aylesbury you got. Even though working boats had beaten us by twenty years, it felt like a working waterway. But redevelopment has been remorseless and the approach to the terminal basin feels less like the old Aylesbury we knew, and more like Anywhere.

NB: travelling towards Aylesbury from Marsworth, follow the map from right to left.

Bucks. Herts.
Red House Lock
Buckland Lock
Bates
Arla Dairy
Dog House
Broughton Lock
rise of old rly
ACS
Aylesbury Locks
park
Tesco
Kings Head
Thame
wc
wc

Aylesbury
for details of facilities at Aylesbury turn to page 56

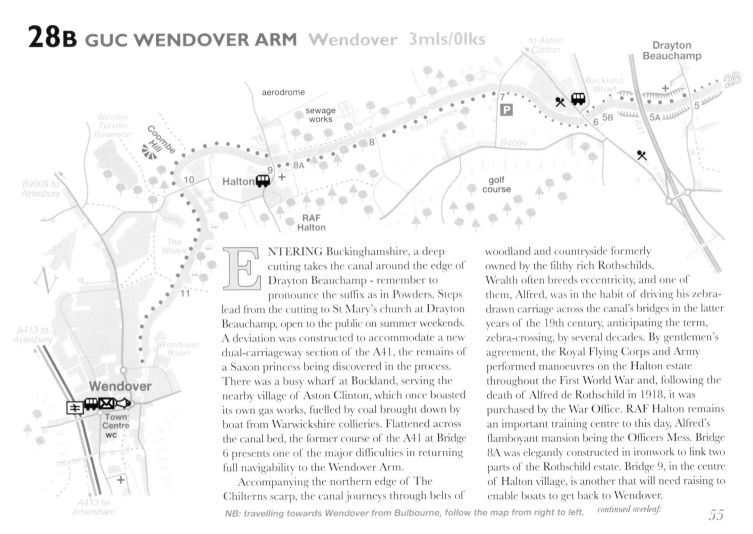

ENTERING Buckinghamshire, a deep cutting takes the canal around the edge of Drayton Beauchamp - remember to pronounce the suffix as in Powders. Steps lead from the cutting to St Mary's church at Drayton Beauchamp, open to the public on summer weekends. A deviation was constructed to accommodate a new dual-carriageway section of the A41, the remains of a Saxon princess being discovered in the process. There was a busy wharf at Buckland, serving the nearby village of Aston Clinton, which once boasted its own gas works, fuelled by coal brought down by boat from Warwickshire collieries. Flattened across the canal bed, the former course of the A41 at Bridge 6 presents one of the major difficulties in returning full navigability to the Wendover Arm.

Accompanying the northern edge of The Chilterns scarp, the canal journeys through belts of woodland and countryside formerly owned by the filthy rich Rothschilds. Wealth often breeds eccentricity, and one of them, Alfred, was in the habit of driving his zebra-drawn carriage across the canal's bridges in the latter years of the 19th century, anticipating the term, zebra-crossing, by several decades. By gentlemen's agreement, the Royal Flying Corps and Army performed manoeuvres on the Halton estate throughout the First World War and, following the death of Alfred de Rothschild in 1918, it was purchased by the War Office. RAF Halton remains an important training centre to this day, Alfred's flamboyant mansion being the Officers Mess. Bridge 8A was elegantly constructed in ironwork to link two parts of the Rothschild estate. Bridge 9, in the centre of Halton village, is another that will need raising to enable boats to get back to Wendover.

NB: travelling towards Wendover from Bulbourne, follow the map from right to left. *continued overleaf:*

continued from page 55:

Weston Turville Reservoir was built to compensate millers whose water supply had been diverted to feed the canal. There are views, westwards, to Coombe Hill topped by a memorial to the 148 men of Buckinghamshire who lost their lives in the Second Boer War. The Wides are reedy expanses of water inhabited by dragonflies and water fowl. At one time RAF Halton was linked to the Metropolitan & Great Central Joint Railway, which runs through Wendover, by a branch line which crossed the canal where footbridge No.11 now stands. The original railway bridge was erected by German prisoners of war.

Somewhat anticlimactically, the arm ends abruptly in what might unkindly be called a swamp, but is in fact just a long ago silted-up terminal basin. The quacking of resident ducks, 'noises off' from the neighbouring school playground, and the plashing over a little weir of the stream which feeds the arm create an agreeable soundtrack; a coda to a little canal of considerable beauty.

Aylesbury   Map 28A

You shouldn't (necessarily) judge a book by its cover, a person by their appearance, or - in Aylesbury's case - a town by its egregious inner ring-road which appears hell-bent on throttling the life out of what is rather a nice place, if you manage to make it across the road in one piece. Notwithstanding its status as the county town of Buckinghamshire, Aylesbury is comparatively small. It became an administrative centre when Buckingham was partially destroyed by fire in 1725. The sloping market place, with its cobbles, statues, clocktower and sturdy municipal buildings, sets the tone. Further on, threading attractive lanes and alleyways, you come upon the substantial parish church of St Mary's - the highest and probably the most peaceful point in Aylesbury.

Eating & Drinking

THE DOG HOUSE - Broughton Lane. Tel: 01296 485228. Country pub reached from Br. 15. HP22 5AR
THE FARMERS' BAR - Market Square. Tel: 01296 718812. The historic King's Head Inn belongs to the National Trust, but this charming bar is operated by the local Chiltern Brewery (whose lovely Beechwood bitter comes served in foaming tankards) and you can either eat and drink within its comfortably furnished interior or spill out onto the courtyard. *Good Beer Guide* listed. HP20 2RW

Shopping

The town centre is a five minute walk from the canal basin. Two indoor precincts are occupied by most household names. Markets on Wed, Fri & Sat; Farmers' Market on the fourth Tuesday of the month. Tesco by Lock 16, Waitrose beside Waterside Theatre, Morrisons by the railway station. PO in W. H. Smith. Launderette at the foot of High Street.

Things to Do

TOURIST INFORMATION CENTRE - King's Head, Market Square. Tel: 01296 330559. HP20 2RW
BUCKINGHAMSHIRE COUNTY MUSEUM - Church Street. Tel: 01296 331441. Admission free. Local history and a gallery devoted to Roald Dahl. HP20 2QP
WATERSIDE THEATRE - Exhange Street. Tel: 0844 871 7607. Imposing venue handily placed for visiting boaters. HP20 1UG

Connections

BUSES - Arriva service 61 runs usefully for towpathers via Bulbourne (Map 28) to Dunstable and Luton hourly Mon-Sat. Tel: 0871 200 2233.
TRAINS - Chiltern Trains to/from London Marylebone. Enthusiasts will relish the branchline ride to Princes Risborough operated at certain times by a 1960 vintage single unit railcar. Tel: 08457 484950.
TAXIS - Five Twos. Tel: 01296 422222.

Wendover   Map 28B

Two transport infrastructure projects are of over-riding concern to this pretty little town on the edge of the Chilterns: yes, they would welcome their boats back; no, they don't want HS2 on their doorstep. If you've energy after the arm, follow the Ridgeway to the monument-capped summit of Coombe Hill

Eating & Drinking

LE BISTRO - Pound Street. Tel: 01296 622092. Appealing little restaurant open for lunch from noon Thur-Sun, and dinner from 6pm Tue-Sat. HP22 6EJ
McCOY'S - High Street. Tel: 01296 708243. Fish & chip shop and restaurant. HP22 6EA
WENDOVER POINT - High Street. Tel: 01296 696380. Italian restaurant from 10am daily. HP22 6EA
Wide choice of other restaurants, cafes and pubs.

Shopping

Quaint little shopping centre with a good wine shop/ deli (No.2) on Pound Street. Budgens on High Street. Several antiques/crafts outlets, and a local produce market on the 3rd Saturday in the month.

Connections

BUSES - Arriva service 50 operates half-hourly, Mon-Sat (and 2/3 times on Suns) to/from Aylesbury.
TRAINS - as Aylesbury. Tel: 08457 484950.
TAXIS - Call a Cab. Tel: 01296 580506.

TRING'S three mile summit section extends from Bulbourne to Cowroast. As the canal emerges from Tring Cutting there are glimpses eastwards above the beechwoods to the urn-topped column which stands on Aldbury Common, about a mile and a half east of Tring railway station. Anyone with an empathy for canal history is honour bound to make a pilgrimage on foot to pay homage to this monument, erected in 1832 in memory of the doyen of canal promoters, Francis Egerton, the third Duke of Bridgewater. Inside the column a staircase climbs to a viewing balcony two hundred feet up. The neighbouring estate of Ashridge (where Graham Greene was wont to play Russian roulette as a bored young man) was one of the Canal Duke's properties, albeit one that he allowed to fall into ruin.

A significant enough boating centre now, in working boat days Cowroast was the location of a control office for correlating boat movements up and down the Grand Union. Southbound travellers commence their descent to the Thames at Brentford in the charming company of the River Bulbourne, a little chalk stream once noted for its watercress. It's worth pausing at Northchurch to visit St Mary's church, and the simple grave (by the porch) of 'Peter the Wild Boy', an 18th century curiosity. Gas Locks recall the existence of Berkhamsted Gasworks from which Clayton's tanker boats

Berk-hamsted once collected tar destined for refining at Oldbury in the Black Country. Tennis courts herald the approach to Berkhamsted, a supremely civilised town which clearly takes a pride in the appearance of its canal and, by the same token, creates a favourable impression with canallers be they on foot or afloat. Graffiti and vandalism are conspicuously absent as the canal moves agreeably along its corridor between the railway and the Roman's Akeman Street. From beds in the chalky Bulbourne, bundles of watercress were floated downstream in little vessels for loading onto trains at Berkhamsted station. Berkhamsted FC's petite football stadium lies in the vicinity of Lock 53. The club can trace its roots back to the end of the First World War when returning soldiers formed a club known as The Comrades. A series of attractive metal plaques interpret local history, from which you derive many gems: such as that in 1852 a man from

continued overleaf:

paths to B'water Monument

Aldbury

Northchurch Common

Northchurch Tunnels

R. Bulbourne

Northchurch

Dudswell

Cowroast Marina

B'water Mon.

TRING SUMMIT 391ft asl

Cowroast

Town Centre

Waitrose

castle

Locks
46 Cowroast Lock 6ft 0ins
47 & 48 Dudswell Locks 13ft 4ins
49 & 50 Northchurch Locks 13ft 7ins
51 & 52 Gas Locks 13ft 4ins
53 Berkhamsted Lock 5ft 10ins
54 Ravens Lane Lock 5ft 8ins
55 Rising Sun Lock 5ft 4ins

continued from page 57:

Clun in Shropshire set up a works in Berkhamsted to manufacture the world's first commercially produced sheep-dip from arsenic and sulphur. A canalside totem pole (genuine and imported from Canada by the owner of a timber yard which stood on the site before it was redeveloped for housing) creates extra interest as the canal passes within an arrow's flight of the impressive motte & bailey remains of Berkhamsted Castle. Geoffrey Chaucer was Clerk of Works here and Thomas Becket the castle's Constable at one time. In more recent times the town's most famous citizen (Ed Reardon notwithstanding) has been Graham Greene who was born in 1904, his father being a housemaster - and subsequently headmaster - of Berkhamsted School, a substantial campus encountered by canallers walking to the High Street from Bridge 141: the chapel organ was playing last time we passed. The canal is mentioned in a number of Greene's works, and he autobiographically recalls 'that odd gritty smell blowing up from the coal barges' and fictionally 'the smell of wet leaves and canal water'.

Below Rising Sun Lock the Bulbourne joins the canal briefly, being the first of several flings with rivers that the Grand Union experiences between Berkhamsted and Uxbridge.

Cowroast   Map 29

Nothing to do with bovine barbecues, but a corruption of 'cow rest', a throwback to cattle droving.

Eating & Drinking

THE COW ROAST - Cowroast (A4251 - access from Bridge 137). Tel: 01442 822287. Well known pub under new ownership. HP23 5RF

Connections

BUSES - Arriva service 500 operates half-hourly (see service 501 on Suns) to/from Aylesbury and Watford along the Grand Union corridor. Tel: 0871 200 2233.

Aldbury   Map 29

Thatch, flint, stocks and a duckpond: a little bit of heaven come loose and landed in Hertfordshire. A congenial base camp for your assault on the fiendish north face of the Bridgewater Monument

Eating & Drinking

THE GREYHOUND - Stock Road. Tel: 01442 851228. Well-appointed Hall & Woodhouse (of Dorset) inn offering bar/restaurant food and accommodation. Open from 11am daily. HP23 5RT

THE VALIANT TROOPER - Trooper Road. Tel: 01442 851203. Village local. HP23 5RW

Shopping

Well stocked post office stores.

Things to Do

ASHRIDGE ESTATE - National Trust beechwoods. Tel: 01442 851227. Access to Bridgewater Monument at weekends Apr-Oct. Shop and cafe. HP4 1LT.

Connections

BUSES - service 387 operates bi-hourly (not Sun) to/from Tring via railway station. Tel: 0871 200 2233.

Berkhamsted   Map 29

It always seems to be sunny when we pass through 'Berko'. Or perhaps that's just the demeanor of its inhabitants. 19th century Berkhamsted was a centre of straw-plaiting for the hatmakers of Dunstable and Luton. Now it's a vibrant residential town with a tree-lined, traffic-calmed High Street, a most pleasant place for sauntering, window-shopping or just 'promenading' on summer evenings in search of Ed, Jaz, Felix and Ping.

Eating & Drinking

THE BOAT - Bridge 142. Tel: 01442 877152. A modern Fullers pub, photographs of Graham Greene adorn one wall. Nice canalside terrace. HP4 2EF

BRASSERIE BLANC - 262 High Street. Tel: 01442 285480. Breakfast from 9am daily; lunch from noon; dinner from 5.30pm. HP4 1AQ

CARLUCCIO'S - 196 High Street. Tel: 01442 877807. Chain inspired by Antonio Carluccio of *Two Greedy Italians* fame. This one's prettily housed in Berko's town hall and tables spill out onto the pavement. Open 8am-11pm daily (9am on Suns). HP4 3BA

HOUSE OF HIGH TEA - 61 High Street. Tel: 01442 871905. Sweet little tea room. HP4 2DE

THE OLIVE TREE - 270 High Street. Tel: 01442 876726. Friendly family-owned eatery. HP4 1AQ

RISING SUN - Canalside (Lock 55). Tel: 01442 864913. Lively *Good Beer Guide* listed pub nicknamed 'The Riser' with beers from the Tring Brewery. HP4 2EG

Shopping

Berkhamsted's little shops are full of character and include Eastwoods butchers (who make pretty good pork pies - for the south!), handily placed for canallers by Bridge 142. Waitrose have a supermarket above Lock 53 with visitor moorings adjacent. Street Markets on Wed & Sat. Farmers Market 3rd Sun.

Connections

BUSES - Arriva service 500 as Cowroast.

TRAINS - frequent trains between London Euston, Milton Keynes and Northampton, calling at Tring, Cheddington and Leighton Buzzard specifically, who knows, for the benefit of towpath walkers. Tel: 08457 484950.

TAXIS - Dacorum Cars - Tel: 01442 872872.

CANALS - as sooner or later we all discover to our cost; financial or emotional - are contagious. One July evening in 1948, Tim Wilkinson got talking to a working boatman at the Fishery Inn, Boxmoor. The next thing he knew, he and his wife were steering the pair *Chiswick* and *Bawtry* hell for leather up and down the Grand Union with cargoes of timber, steel, meat powder and wood pulp as entertainingly recounted in *Hold on a Minute*, one of the earliest authentic accounts of what it was like to work on the canals, and a good read to accompany you along the Grand Union.

Sewer (or Sewerage) Lock lives olfactorily up to its name. Canals appear to have a baffling predilection for sewage works; though perhaps, somewhat unnervingly, it's the other way round. The Bulbourne looks far too clear and innocent to be associated with such murky waters. When it wasn't nuturing watercress, it powered watermills. At Winkwell, the picturesque, weatherboarded heart of one of the river's old corn mills is entombed within a modern hotel and restaurant.

Joseph Buck, the lock-keeper at Winkwell, went to a watery grave in the canal on Christmas Day 1898, probably as a result of too much festive spirit. The death toll was unfortunately much higher here on 30th September 1945 when the Perth-Euston sleeper came off the rails and hurtled down the embankment, snuffing out forty-three lives in the process. The river joins the canal briefly again at the tail of Lock 61 and together they perform an S-bend beneath the railway, the graceful ironwork of Robert Stephenson's original bridge for the London & Birmingham Railway having been unforgivably coated in concrete. Watercress beds were commercially worked between the canal and the railway until the 1980s. Fishery Inn still offers refreshment to boaters, but few of them can be described as 'working'. An Arcadian interlude ensues as the canal glides across Boxmoor, an area of chestnut-shaded meadowland which retains its ancient grazing rights. It was from a chestnut tree that Robert Snooks was hung in 1802, the last man to be executed for highway robbery in England. Two stones mark his likely resting place. The Bulbourne joins the Gade at Hemel Hempstead; the latter briefly crossing the canal. Lime juice, transhipped at London Docks, was delivered by narrowboat to the wharf by Bridge 151 (now occupied by B&Q) for Roses, the cordial makers, until 1981.

⚠ Swing-bridge 147 is electrically operated and you will need a CART facilities key to access the control panel.

Locks
56 Top Side Lock 8ft 0ins
57 Bottom side Lock 8ft 6ins
58 Sewer Lock 6ft 1in
59-61 Winkwell Locks 20ft 4ins

Locks
62 Boxmoor Top Lock 6ft 8ins
63 Fishery Lock 7ft 1in
64 Boxmoor Lock 7ft 1in

for details of facilities at Bourne End and Hemel Hempstead turn to page 61

59

31 GRAND UNION CANAL Apsley & Kings Langley 4mls/8lks/3hrs

FEW Grand Union canalscapes have altered quite as fundamentally as Apsley's. Housing and retail developments offer scant evidence of the era when John Dickinson's Apsley Paper Mills employed upwards of five thousand folk in buildings which pressed in upon the canal for half a mile. Arms led off the main channel into covered loading bays where powered craft would position themselves carefully under ventilation cones so as to preserve a relatively clean and fumeless environment. Coal was discharged on the east bank of the canal and ferried across to the furnaces via a corrugated-iron clad conveyor. The sense of purposeful activity must have been intense. All this came to an abrupt halt - as far as canal carrying was concerned - in 1963 when, by NCB diktat, the mill began to source its coal from a colliery not connected to the inland waterways. The manufacture of paper continued until production was transferred away and the works were demolished in the early 'nineties.

Apsley's paper industry can trace its origins to the Fourdrinier brothers operations at the end of the 18th century. Apsley, Nash and Home Park mills further developed under the stewardship of John Dickinson & Co. An express boat service known as the 'Paper Mill Dashers' operated between Apsley and Dickinson's warehouses in Paddington, eight hours being taken to cover 35 miles and 23 locks! The relationship between the mill owners and the canal company was not necessarily harmonious in the early days of the Grand Junction. Problems with water supplies to the mills necessitated construction of a canal deviation in 1819. Between bridges 152 and 158 a new course to the south of the original was adopted, incorporating a length of the River Gade, whilst four relatively deep and water-wasteful locks were replaced by five shallower ones; hence 69A at Kings Langley.

Last owned by a South African company, Nash Mills closed in 2006, and the site has been redeveloped for housing. Below Nash Locks the canalised River Gade drifts picturesquely through a wide overlooked by tall poplar trees. Not all the mills in the area made paper. Toovey's Mill which stood by Bridge 157, produced flour from wheat brought up from Brentford by boat. Another well known source of traffic for the canal was the Ovaltine works adjacent to Bridge 158. Sadly the factory, opened in 1913, closed in 2002 when production of the famous bedtime drink was transferred to Switzerland. The company operated their own fleet of narrowboats apparelled in an eye-catching advertising livery, and even had a dairy and an egg farm in florid half-timber on the neighbouring hillside. The Art Deco works has been incorporated in a new housing scheme, though it is necessary to go round to the other side of it to appreciate its former glory.

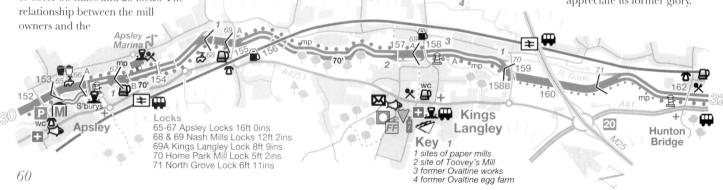

Locks
65-67 Apsley Locks 16ft 0ins
68 & 69 Nash Mills Locks 12ft 2ins
69A Kings Langley Lock 8ft 9ins
70 Home Park Mill Lock 5ft 2ins
71 North Grove Lock 6ft 11ins

Key
1 sites of paper mills
2 site of Toovey's Mill
3 former Ovaltine works
4 former Ovaltine egg farm

Bourne End Map 30

The tiny Victorian church near Bridge 145 is the work of George Gilbert Scott, a project marginally less challenging than the Midland Grand Hotel at St Pancras.

Eating & Drinking

THREE HORSESHOES - Bridge 147. Tel: 01442 862585. Picturesque 16th century pub which predates its canal setting. Open from noon daily. HP1 2RZ
WHITE HORSE - London Road. Tel: 01442 863888. Comfortable pub owned by Hertfordshire's oldest independent brewers, McMullen & Sons. Wide range of food. HP1 2RH

Connections

BUSES - Arriva service 500 operates half-hourly (service 501 on Suns) to/from Aylesbury and Watford along the Grand Union corridor. Tel: 0871 200 2233.

Hemel Hempstead Map 30

Eras come and go. The lofty Kodak building no longer defines Hemel economically or culturally. Kodak, Kojak? Yesterday's names for yesterdays' people. Hemel's 1960s new town architecture comes over as cutting edge as Dan Dare now. Glimpsed between Boxmoor's chestnuts it could be Anytown UK. But walking through the new Riverside shopping development into Marlowes, you experience architectural history unpeeling itself. And by the time you reach the human scale of the old town (where, incidentally, aficionados of *Pie in the Sky* will spot Henry Crabbe's restaurant) all's well with the world.

Eating & Drinking

FISHERY INN - Bridge 149. Tel: 01442 230197. Well known canalside inn, comfortably refurbished. Open daily from 11am (noon Suns). HP1 1NA
K2 - Balti restaurant alongside Bridge 151. Tel: 01442 239993. Mountainous portions? HP1 1NA

SEATTLE STEAK HOUSE - St John's Road. Tel: 01442 264846. Just across the cricket ground from the canal. Juicy steaks for famished boaters. HP1 1JR

Shopping

Riverside and Marlowes shopping centres. Aldi supermarket just south-west of Bridge 151.

Connections

BUSES - service 500/501 as Bourne End.
TRAINS - frequent London Midland stopping services between London Euston, Watford and Milton Keynes etc. Tel: 08457 484950.

Apsley Map 31

Once the papermaking seat of John Dickinson's worldwide empire, now a rather lacklustre satellite of Hemel Hempstead made up of apartment blocks and business parks, one known - presumably with unintentional irony - as Doolittle Meadows.

Eating & Drinking

CALZONE - Dickinson Quay. Tel: 01442 265100. Pizzas, open 10am-10.30pm (6.30pm Sun). HP3 9WG.
MARINA SPICE LOUNGE - Dickinson Quay. Tel: 01442 270603. Indian restaurant and take-away. HP3 9WQ
THE PAPER MILL - Stationers Place (Bridge 153B). Tel: 01442 288800. Fuller's new-build pub open daily from 10am. Canalside patio. HP3 9RH
WOODYS - Dickinson Quay. Tel: 01442 266280. Cosy canalside vegetarian cafe/restaurant for soups, salads, crepes and pizzas. Open daily 10am-10pm (5pm Suns). HP3 9WG

Shopping

Convenience store at Apsley Marina. Large Sainsbury's (with handy offside moorings) by Bridge 153A.

Things to Do

FROGMORE PAPER MILL - Fourdrinier Way. Tel: 01442 234600. Paper is a subject close to the

Pearson/Wayzgoose publishing heart, and this lovely little museum deserves to be visited and lingered over by anyone for whom paper still matters. Visitor centre tours Thur, Fri, Sun & BH Mons. Cafe, gallery and shop daily ex Sat 11am-4.30pm. Thursday boat trips April-September. Best access via Bridge152. HP3 9RY

Connections

BUSES - service 500/501 as Bourne End.
TRAINS - London Midland as Hemel Hempstead.

Kings Langley Map 31

Unusually, Kings Langley looks better by road than by boat. Suburban infills are responsible for this, but the High Street, strung agreeably out along the old London to Aylesbury road, is worth investigating. Nicholas Breakspear, the only Englishman to become Pope, was born at nearby Bedmond circa 1100, whilst Piers Gaveston (Edward II's favourite) was buried at the Priory, now part of the Rudolf Steiner School.

Eating & Drinking

FRED & GINGER - High Street. Tel: 01923 262420. Stylish coffee shop open from 8am daily (9am Suns) for salads, sandwiches, cakes etc. WD4 9HT
KINGS LANGLEY TANDOORI - High Street. Tel: 01923 270668. Indian restaurant open from 5pm daily (1pm Sun). WD4 8AB
OSCARS - High Street. Tel: 01923 263800. 'Innovative pizzas'! and other Mediterranean dishes. Open noon to 10.30pm daily. WD4 8AB

Shopping

A good choice of shops including a butcher, two pharmacies, post office, Spar convenience store, off licence and launderette. Dalling & Co is an excellent delicatessen/cafe and wine merchant.

Connections

BUSES - service 500/501 as Bourne End.
TRAINS - London Midland as Hemel Hempstead.

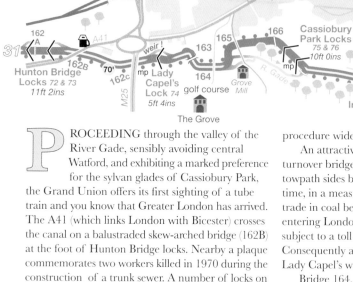

PROCEEDING through the valley of the River Gade, sensibly avoiding central Watford, and exhibiting a marked preference for the sylvan glades of Cassiobury Park, the Grand Union offers its first sighting of a tube train and you know that Greater London has arrived. The A41 (which links London with Bicester) crosses the canal on a balustraded skew-arched bridge (162B) at the foot of Hunton Bridge locks. Nearby a plaque commemorates two workers killed in 1970 during the construction of a trunk sewer. A number of locks on this canal retain their DIS, or distance, posts located equidistantly above and below each lock. In the event of boats approaching a lock simultaneously from opposite directions, the first to reach the distance post had preference for use of the lock. The captains of horse-drawn boats would crack their whip to signify reaching the post, in the motor boat era a klaxon could be used, but it was obviously an operating procedure wide open to abuse!

An attractive whitewashed turnover bridge effects a change in towpath sides below Lady Capel's Lock. At one time, in a measure taken to protect the maritime trade in coal between Tyneside and London, coal entering London from the north and west was subject to a toll taken on the Hertfordshire border. Consequently a good deal of coal was unloaded at Lady Capel's wharf so as to escape the tax.

Bridge 164, providing access to The Grove, an 18th century mansion on the neighbouring hillside, was ornamented at the request of the local landowner whose grounds have become a ubiquitous golf course. The former water mill at Grove has been converted for residential use. Between locks 76 and 77 the canal again adopts the course of the River Gade. As it moves through Cassiobury Park - scene of the 2013 National Waterways Festival - the canal becomes a popular haunt for strolls and picnics. A marina occupies the site of Cassio Bridge wharf which served Watford. Those London Underground trains rattle across the high bridge of the Metropolitan Railway. Scarcely less imposing, but surreptitiously abandoned by default in the 'nineties, the old London & North Western Railway branch to Croxley Green spans the canal south of Bridge 169 by way of a substantial girder bridge. There are plans for it to be re-opened, though they have been lying in some civil servant's in-tray for a discouragingly long time. A number of interesting former working boats tend to congregate hereabouts, recalling the days when Croxley Paper Mills were the last to receive regular deliveries of coal by narrowboat, around 1970. Widebeam boats brought cargoes of esparto grass up from Brentford. With a certain inevitability, the site is now covered by new housing.

Squat tube trains rub shoulders with their altogether taller Chiltern Trains cousins on the railway bridge above Lot Mead Lock. At its tail, the River Gade briefly joins the canal for the last occasion before it becomes the River Colne, which rises to the south of St Albans, having accommodated, en route, the River Ver. Some charming, not to say eccentric residential craft are moored below Lot Mead Lock. The abandoned Watford & Rickmansworth railway - electrified as early as 1927 - has become a popular traffic-free path for walkers, cyclists and horse-riders known as the Ebury Way after Lord Ebury of Moor Park who promoted the railway. Its passenger services acquired the delightful sobriquet of 'watercress trains' as they were often used to carry the locally grown commodity to Watford market. Electrified or not, the line closed to passenger services in 1952. It is, however, not unknown for itinerant guide book writers to walk along its trackbed imitating the sounds of vanished electric trains.

Watford   Map 32

There are despondent moments when you can appreciate how Novgorod came to be one of Watford's twin towns. Where once was Home Counties gentility, now is global banality. You don't need to be a native to lament this evisceration. There was a time when towns like Watford were defined by their industries. But where are the equivalents of Benskins, Scammell, and the photogravure giants Odhams and Sun Engraving now? Camelot? Exactly! Yet you can forgive anything, strolling through Cassiobury's splendid park on a sunny day, hoping that you're not too middle-aged to sample the miniature railway. And those with a Pearsonesque eye for the overlooked will find solace in flinty St Mary's (and its Morison monuments); RC Holy Rood (by the architect of Westminster Cathedral); Palace Theatre (of 1908); the Boys Grammar School (where *The History Boys* was filmed); and Rembrandt House, erstwhile home of the Sun print and engraving works.

Eating & Drinking

TARBOUSH - Market Street. Tel: 01923 248898. Zany Lebanese cafe open 11am-midnight daily. Tarboush means fez! WD18 0PR
PEPE ROSSO - High Street. Tel: 01923 241414. Homely, authentic Italian. WD17 2EN
SPICE LOUNGE - Market Street. Tel: 01923 236500. Highly regarded Indian restaurant. WD18 0PY
CHA CHA CHA - Cassiobury Park. Tel: 01923 247868. Charming little cafe in parkland setting, open from 10am daily. WD18 7HY
RISING SUN - Ascot Road (near Bridge 169). Tel: 01923 281185. Brewers Fayre, opens for breakfast from 6.30am (7 on Suns). WD18 8AP

Shopping

It's a brisk quarter of an hour's walk from the canal to the town centre. The Harlequin/Intu is the magnet for most shoppers, but the cognoscenti head for the splendid indoor market which rolls up its shutters on Tue, Thur, Fri & Sat.

Things to Do

WATFORD MUSEUM - High Street. Tel: 01923 232297. Imposingly housed in what were once the offices of Benskins Brewery. Local history and art, notably the paintings of Gordon Hales (1916-1997) who lived in the town for much of his life and specialised in evocative maritime and Thames river scenes. WD17 2DT

Connections

BUSES - Arriva services 500/550 operate usefully, northwards along the Grand Union corridor for towpath walkers. Carousel service 336 and Green Line 724 link Watford with Ricky. Tel: 0871 200 2233.
TRAINS - Virgin, London Midland and Southern services from Watford Junction, about 25 mins walk east of the canal. Tel: 08457 484950.
TUBE - Metropolitan Line services to/from central London from terminus adjacent Cassiobury Park. Tel: 0843 222 1234.
TAXIS - Cassio Cars. Tel: 01923 803603.

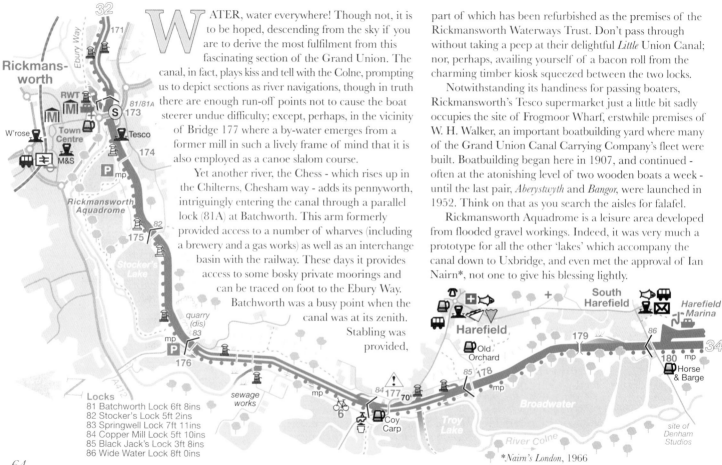

WATER, water everywhere! Though not, it is to be hoped, descending from the sky if you are to derive the most fulfilment from this fascinating section of the Grand Union. The canal, in fact, plays kiss and tell with the Colne, prompting us to depict sections as river navigations, though in truth there are enough run-off points not to cause the boat steerer undue difficulty; except, perhaps, in the vicinity of Bridge 177 where a by-water emerges from a former mill in such a lively frame of mind that it is also employed as a canoe slalom course.

Yet another river, the Chess - which rises up in the Chilterns, Chesham way - adds its pennyworth, intriguingly entering the canal through a parallel lock (81A) at Batchworth. This arm formerly provided access to a number of wharves (including a brewery and a gas works) as well as an interchange basin with the railway. These days it provides access to some bosky private moorings and can be traced on foot to the Ebury Way. Batchworth was a busy point when the canal was at its zenith. Stabling was provided,

part of which has been refurbished as the premises of the Rickmansworth Waterways Trust. Don't pass through without taking a peep at their delightful *Little* Union Canal; nor, perhaps, availing yourself of a bacon roll from the charming timber kiosk squeezed between the two locks.

Notwithstanding its handiness for passing boaters, Rickmansworth's Tesco supermarket just a little bit sadly occupies the site of Frogmoor Wharf, erstwhile premises of W. H. Walker, an important boatbuilding yard where many of the Grand Union Canal Carrying Company's fleet were built. Boatbuilding began here in 1907, and continued - often at the atonishing level of two wooden boats a week - until the last pair, *Aberystwyth* and *Bangor*, were launched in 1952. Think on that as you search the aisles for falafel.

Rickmansworth Aquadrome is a leisure area developed from flooded gravel workings. Indeed, it was very much a prototype for all the other 'lakes' which accompany the canal down to Uxbridge, and even met the approval of Ian Nairn*, not one to give his blessing lightly.

Locks
81 Batchworth Lock 6ft 8ins
82 Stocker's Lock 5ft 2ins
83 Springwell Lock 7ft 11ins
84 Copper Mill Lock 5ft 10ins
85 Black Jack's Lock 3ft 8ins
86 Wide Water Lock 8ft 0ins

*Nairn's London, 1966

Out in open country again, Stocker's Lock comes as a piquant reminder of just how pretty a canal can be. The lock-keeper's cottage is particularly lovely, whilst, overlooking Bridge 175, stands Stocker's House, erected for the Collector of Coal Duties when the taxable boundary was moved closer to London than its original location north of Watford. Stocker's Farm features a handsome cluster of weatherboarded barns and stables.

In littoral mood, the canal proceeds boskily towards Uxbridge. A monkey hangs disconsolately from the ruins of a derelict cement works. Colne Valley sewage plant received its last delivery of coal by Willow Wren in 1969. The substantial industrial premises by Lock 84 have variously produced corn, copper, paper, asbestos and rubber. Those canoeists slalom in the choppy cross-currents below the lock.

Rickmansworth   Map 33

'Ricky' in the local patois is the sort of place one imagines Just William growing timelessly up in. In that respect it is a typical small Home Counties town, self-sufficient despite its obvious proximity to London. William Penn (of Pennsylvania) and George Eliot were both sometime residents. The churchyard of St Mary the Virgin provides an attractive route into the town and sets the tone for what follows.

Eating & Drinking
CAFE IN THE PARK - Frogmoor Lane, the Aquadrome. Tel: 01923 711131. WD3 1NB
THE FEATHERS - Church Street. Tel: 01923 770081. Comfortable 'public house and kitchen' open from noon, easily reached from Bridge 173. WD3 1DJ
LEMONGRASS - Church Street. Tel: 01923 776779. Thai restaurant. WD3 1BU
MAURIZIO'S - Church Street. Tel: 01923 775701. Homely Italian restaurant. WD3 1BX
RASAL BRASSERIE - High Street. Tel: 01923 778722. Indian restaurant. WD3 1AY
ZAZA - Church Street. Tel: 01923 772287. Stylish Italian restaurant. Al fresco opportunities, weather permitting. WD3 1DE

Shopping
Large Tesco with customer moorings on off side between bridges 173 & 174, but much nicer to visit the town centre's traditional shops 5 minutes walk from Batchworth Lock. At the west end of High Street there's a Marks & Spencers, whilst up by the railway station there's a branch of Waitrose. Dickins wine merchants (at the east end of High Street) were established in 1949.

Things to Do
BATCHWORTH LOCK CANAL CENTRE - Church Street. Tel: 01923 778382. Keep your eyes peeled for *Roger*, a preserved narrowboat usually moored in the vicinity under the auspices of Rickmansworth Waterway Trust. *Roger* dates from 1936 and was built (not locally by Walkers, but) by Bushells at Tring (see Map 28) for Harvey-Taylor, an Aylesbury canal carrier. Towards the end of its career it worked for Samuel Barlow and Blue Line and was withdrawn from service in 1968. WD3 1JD
THREE RIVERS MUSEUM - Basing House, High Street. Tel: 01923 775882. Small (but beautiful) displays of local history in the land of Chess, Gade and Colne. Open 2-4pm Mon-Fri and 10am-4pm Sat. Admission free. Worth it just to hear the volunteers unselfconsciously reminiscing among themselves. WD3 1RL

Connections
BUSES - Green Line service 724 operates hourly (bi-hourly Suns) between Heathrow and Harlow, three hours apart! For canal explorers it provides a useful link through Rickmansworth and Denham and between Watford and Uxbridge. Arriva service 320 links Ricky with Hemel Hempstead via Watford half-hourly (hourly Suns). Tel: 0871 200 2233.

TRAINS - Chiltern Trains serve Ricky on their way between London Marylebone and Aylesbury. Tel: 08457 484950. And, of course, it's also on London Underground's Metropolitan Line: Tel: 0343 222 1234.
TAXIS - Boughtons & Eagles. Tel: 01923 896060.

Harefield   Map 33

Former Middlesex village notable for its heart and lung hospital. The isolated parish church of St Mary contains some astonishing monuments, whilst in its graveyard lie over a hundred Australians who died from their injuries at the hospital during the Great War. Bus U9 connects frequently with Uxbridge.

Eating & Drinking
OLD ORCHARD - Park Lane (just uphill from Lock 85). Tel: 01895 822631. Formerly Edwinns restaurant, now part of the excellent Brunning & Price group. After a bottle or two of Pinot Grigio on the terrace, the Broadwater below is very easily mistaken for Lake Garda in the Italian Alps. UB9 6HJ
COY CARP - canalside Bridge 177. Tel: 01895 821471. Comfortably furnished Vintage Inns pub/restaurant. Landlord/London Pride. UB9 6HZ
HORSE & BARGE - adjacent Wide Water Lock. Tel: 01895 834806. Family pub with large garden. Opens noon daily. UB9 6PE

Shopping
Co-op, Spar, baker, butcher and pharmacy about quarter of an hour's walk uphill from Black Jack's Lock.

34 GRAND UNION CANAL Uxbridge 4mls/2lks/2hrs

T HE Grand Junction Canal had the Colne Valley pretty much to itself for well over a century before the Great Western and Great Central railway companies collaborated to build a new line through the Chilterns to speed up their respective services between London, the midlands and the north. *Deja Vu?* Denham's imposing blue-brick viaduct spans the canal less than half a mile south of where it is intended that a new bridge will be built to carry HS2 high across the valley. One doubts if the railway barons of the early 20th century experienced even a fraction of the antipathy directed towards the government's 21st century high speed railway aspirations. The irony is that all those 'Metroland' Englishmen's Castles in the Chilterns would not be there at all if the railways had not precipitated such a huge surge in house building. Hey ho, on the world marches, and progress is not easily thwarted. We live in the age allotted to us, whether we find it conducive or not. HS2 protesters? They could do worse than take their cue from the Colne Valley's 18th century millers

who coerced the Grand Junction into building an aqueduct over Fray's River and providing the canal's deepest lock at Denham, so as not to affect the flow of current to their watermills. The setting is so idyllic now, you'd hardly guess at the controversy surrounding the canal's construction. Peace reigns supreme and can be enhanced by venturing off the canal into the bosky glades and marshy meadows of Denham Country Park, a timeless environment where controversy is kept firmly in its place.

It was disappointing to see that the aggregates traffic between Denham and West Drayton, a welcome feature of the last two or three editions of this guide, had ceased. The regular passage of working boats fostered a sense of credibility to this part of the canal absent since the end of the 1960s. It was a relief to learn that the traffic ceased because the gravel pit was worked out, rather than because of any perceived weakness in the notion of water transport. The bland business parks of Uxbridge barely impinge upon the canal's *savoir faire*. Apartments have replaced the flour mill which once overlooked Uxbridge Lock, source of the brand 'Kingsmill'. Uxbridge Boat Centre occupies premises which once belonged to the famous canal carrying company Fellows, Morton & Clayton.

A40 to London

crse of GWR
Uxbridge High St. branch

Denham
Deep
Lock 87
11ft 1ins

181   182   183

mp

33

R. Colne

golf
course

Denham
Country
Park

aggregates
wharf
(disused)

wc (i) P

site of
Denham
Studios

Denham +

R. Misbourne

Denham
Place

🧺 = Denham Day Boats

1

M40 to the
Midlands

Fray's River

Denham
Marina

Town
Centre

crse of GWR
Uxbridge Vine St. branch

Uxbridge

mp

184
Uxbridge
Lock 88
4ft 7ins

185

A408

Uxbridge
Boat
Centre

187

A4020

A   mp 186

River Colne

New
Denham

business
parks

London Loop

⚠ Beware cross-currents
below Uxbridge Lock

A4007 to
Slough

Denham
Map 34

Horse chestnut and wisteria lend Denham the air of a film set, which is exactly what it is. Alexandra Korda opened his Denham (aka London) Film Studios here in 1936, and if a quintessentially English village was called for on location, Denham did very nicely. The studios closed down in 1952, but Denham's good looks still draw hordes; witness three well-appointed pubs and a restaurant where many villages of this size would now boast none. Plaques inform that the actor Sir John Mills lived at Hills House and that the artists William (and son) Ben Nicholson lived at White Cottage. Flowing down off the Chilterns in the vicinity of Great Missenden, the crystal clear waters of the River Misbourne ripple delightfully through Denham.

Eating & Drinking
FRAN'S TEA GARDEN - Denham Deep Lock. Tel: 01895 271070. Charming canalside tea room. Open daily April-October ex Mon & Tue. UB9 4AF
DA REMO - Village Road. Tel: 01895 832425. Plush Italian. UB9 5BA
Three pubs in the village, and fish & chips by the station.

Shopping
Parade of shops beside the railway station.

Things to Do
DENHAM COUNTRY PARK - Tel: 01895 833375. Excellent information point (also known as the Colne Valley Park Visitor Centre) easily reached from the canal at Denham Deep Lock. Helpful staff provide heaps of local information and suggestions for walking itineraries. Open daily throughout the year. Refreshments. UB9 5PG

Connections
TRAINS - Chiltern Trains services. Tel: 08457 484950.
TAXIS - Station Cars. Tel: 01895 832211.

Uxbridge
Map 34

The most important town in the London Borough of Hillingdon, Uxbridge is a worthwhile stop on any boating itinerary. It was a Parliamentarian garrison town during the Civil War, and Charles I attempted to negotiate a peace treaty here in 1644. The Metropolitan Railway reached Uxbridge in 1904 followed by the Piccadilly Line in 1933, at which time the present handsome tube-train terminus was built. RAF Uxbridge opened in 1917 and Lawrence of Arabia passed through in the guise of Aircraftman Ross. The Battle of Britain was directed from an underground command post at the aerodrome. Nowadays Uxbridge is a busy commercial centre and Brunel University has its home here. Notable buildings include St Margaret's church, the Market House, and the Civic Centre.

Eating & Drinking
NONNA ROSA - High Street. Tel: 01895 233570. Lively Italian to north of town centre. UB8 1JT
HARRIS & HOOLE - Market House. Tel: 01895 811568. Coffee shop housed in the splendid Tuscan-columned market hall. UB8 1JW
Three canalside pubs, plus Nandos, Zizzi, Ask, and Prezzo chains in town centre.

Shopping
The lamentably named 'intu', and Pavilions shopping malls find their antithesis in Windsor Street, a quaint little thoroughfare of interesting shops, not least Barnard's friendly bookshop.

Connections
BUSES - service U9 links Uxbridge with Harefield; 724 runs to/from Ricky and Watford (from stops on York Street); and 7 for Slough. Tel: 0871 200 2233.
TUBE - Tel: 0343 222 1234. Metropolitan and Piccadilly lines' services to/from central London.

Cowley
Map 35

Eating & Drinking
MALT SHOVEL - canalside Bridge 188. Tel: 01895 812797. Vintage Inns pub. UB8 2JE
TOLL HOUSE TEAROOM/BISTRO - canalside Lock 89. Tel: 01895 311641. Breakfasts, lunches, teas, takeaways and bistro evenings. UB8 2JE
THE WATER'S EDGE - canalside Bridge 190. Tel: 01895 440550. Popular restaurant and bar. UB8 2JS

Langley
Map 35A

Students and suburbs, but the church features a private chapel and library and is worth a detour to see, even when locked. Console yourselves by paying homage to the artist/designer Paul Nash who is buried in the churchyard along with his wife Margaret.

Slough
Map 35A

Home of Mars and Horlicks, Slough used to be in Bucks, but is now in Berks, which pretty much defines those responsible. The town centre lies a quarter of an hour's dispiriting walk south of the canal, though there are suburban facilities on the way - not least Gaudio's Polish/Italian delicatessen: apparently 1 in 8 of the local population are of Polish extraction. The station is a fine example of railway architecture, built thus to impress Queen Victoria. One can only speculate as to the effect of the spanking new bus station on our present monarch. Beyond the underpass, the Queensmere and Observatory shopping precincts cater for most aspects of modern life, the latter drawing its name from Slough's associations with the 18th century astronomer, William Herschel. The best thing about the town centre used to be its museum, but that has been moved since our last visit, and appears to have shrunk in the process. It's in the library now!

COWLEY LOCK heralds a lengthy pound, particularly if you're heading for central London; in which case you won't encounter another lock all the way to Paddington. Hallelujah! All around you, Greater London goes about its business, but the Grand Union keeps itself to itself, as only canals can. West of the canal, various watercourses create an enchanting landscape which begs to be delved into and enjoyed discriminatingly: why, there is even a lake called Little Britain - cue some well-honed catchphrases. The Colne at this point divides Buckinghamshire from what used to be Middlesex. The canal is wide and purposeful, but linear mooring slows you down. At Cowley Peachey Junction the Slough Arm slinks off on a five mile journey to a town that has endured its fair share of ridicule from John Betjeman to Ricky Gervais. A trance-inducing sequence of aqueducts carry the arm unostentatiously through a bayou-like zone of watery wilderness.

Unconcerned, the main line bears east, bisecting built-up Yiewsley and West Drayton and running in close attendance with Brunel's Great Western Railway whose advent spelt the end of a hitherto ebullient packet boat operation between Uxbridge and Paddington. The broad gauge GWR's first pair of locomotives, *Vulcan* and *Premier* were built in Liverpool and brought by ship to London Docks before being floated up the canal to West Drayton. All that seems like ancient history as the line is progressively upgraded for its role in CrossRail and the electrification scheme to Bristol and beyond, but it would be nice to get the better of time for a moment and glimpse a copper-capped 'Castle' or a 'King' steaming by in the early throes of its classic journey to the West Country.

Along this length of canal once existed several arms to serve adjoining brickfields and other enterprises: Bentinck Dock, Otter Dock, Pocock's Dock, Cooper's Dock and Eastwood's Dock. In recent years Hanson's aggregates wharf (which adjoins the unnumbered concrete bridge carrying the A408 across the canal) has seen a fair amount of waterborne trade, notably from Denham - as remarked upon on Map 34 - but this traffic appears disappointingly moribund now. Commercial carrying by canal faces so many bureaucratic and financial obstacles that even when started is onerous to maintain; as though the powers-that-be are cynically pronouncing:
'Yeah, but no, but yeah, but ...'

Map labels:
- 199
- 36
- rems of Gramophone factory
- 198
- 196
- mp
- Heathrow Airport Junction
- 195
- 194A
- aggregates wharf
- Pocock's Dock
- mp
- 193
- 34
- Cowley (csd - 1962)
- 188
- 89 Cowley Lock 6ft 6ins
- close of Uxbridge Vine Street branch
- Clisby's Bridge
- mp
- 189
- Cowley Peachey Junction
- A408
- 190
- S
- B
- Tesco
- mp
- Town Centre
- Yiewsley
- Morrisons
- West Drayton
- 191
- 192
- WC
- Little Britain Lake
- B470
- Fray's River
- River Colne
- Iver
- FF
- SLOUGH ARM
- GWR Staines branch
- Colne Brook
- 2A
- mp
- M25
- 35A
- Iver
- N
- 68
- 3

= Packet Boat Marina (BWML/High Line Yachting)

* allow 0.5 hours for this section of the Slough Arm

35A GRAND UNION SLOUGH ARM

ONE of the Great *Little* Canal Journeys of the World, the Slough Arm is unusual in that it post-dates the railway running parallel to it. Brunel's Great Western Railway was opened in 1839, the canal didn't carry its first cargo of bricks until 1882. Bricks were pretty much its be all and end all. Henry VI had a kiln built to provide the bricks for Eton College, but the industry's zenith was in the second half of the 19th century. Bricks were stacked all along the canal bank for loading on to barges and transporting to the construction sites of London's burgeoning suburbs. The brickmakers worked in teams of six and were paid piece-work, around five shillings for every thousand bricks they made. It was seasonal work, summer only, and a beer allowance was a perk of the job, supplied to slake prodigious thirsts.

With its iron overbridges, largely straight alignment, and absence of locks, the arm may remind connoisseurs of remote canal termini of the Cannock Extension. It shares with that West Midland canal, the distinction of a busy boatyard which, as far as Bridge 6 at any rate, brings considerable traffic to the canal. West of here, however, the arm has the character of a quiet backwater, the preserve of fishermen and model boat-builders keen to put their latest creations through their paces. Consequently, it is

somewhat introspectively that the arm proceeds towards its undemonstrative end. Airliners flying in and out of Heathrow provide an aural and aerial backdrop to the proceedings. During the summer months the display of water lilies in the margins of the canal would do justice to an ornamental water garden, though their mere presence emphasises the shallow, unboated nature of the route.

Between mileposts 2 and 4, the towpath forms the boundary of Berkshire with Buckinghamshire, or at least it has done since it was moved north from the Thames by meddlesome politicians in 1974. The large factory between bridges 11 and 12 produces Dulux paint.

Five miles from Cowley Peachey the arm peters out in a Bunyanesque Slough of Despond by a builders merchant's yard; the best part of a mile north of Slough's town centre. It is surprising and regrettable that the opportunity was not taken in the first half of the 20th century to extend the canal into Slough's famous trading estate where new traffics may have been won to prolong transport by water in the London area. Horlicks might then have rivalled Ovaltine in the use of canal transport. Proposals have been aired from time to time to connect the arm to the Thames, a mere two miles away. Such a link would obviate the tideway between Teddington and Brentford.

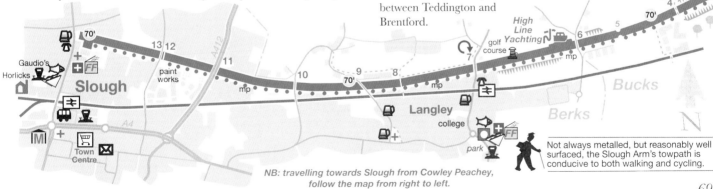

NB: travelling towards Slough from Cowley Peachey, follow the map from right to left.

Not always metalled, but reasonably well surfaced, the Slough Arm's towpath is conducive to both walking and cycling.

BULLS BRIDGE resonates in the hearts and minds of working boat enthusiasts much as Old Oak Common does in those of a railway bent. Working boats foregathered here, pending cargoes, like locomotives awaiting their next turn of duty. The layby where they moored - stern in, bow out - remains evident today, occupied by a motley collection of house boats. A drydock remains in use as well. But other elements of the boat people's past, such as a floating school and a small maternity facility, are merely memories on the canal's emotional compass.

high speed trains roar across the railway bridge as though there were no tomorrow, but on the canal there's time to contemplate all our yesterdays. Proceeding to Brentford and the Thames, pubs pop up at every bridgehole: fathomless thirsts those watermen. Here and there are recreation grounds and distant glimpses of glinting mosques. Adelaide Dock has been purloined by CART for the containment of its maintenance craft. And very well-contained they appear to be.

Opened in 1801, the Paddington Arm heads

The main line of the Grand Union Canal slips down past the remains of His Master's Voice gramophone works, through Hayes towards Brentford, whilst the Paddington Arm disappears through a whitewashed roving bridge on its thirteen, lockless miles to London. Of the fascinating factories which once consorted with the canal, solely Nestle (aka 'Hayes Cocoa' to generations of working boatmen) remains intact, though not, of course, the recipient of coal consignments anymore. Hurrying out of Paddington for the West Country,

disconcertingly northwards, as though determined to return you to Braunston like an unsigned for delivery. Presumably that was never the case regarding Kearley & Tonge's weekly cargo of North Warwickshire coal, the Grand Union's final long distance traffic, last unloaded at the 'Jam 'Ole' in August, 1970. Southall Gas Works is a brownfield site awaiting redevelopment, in the meantime it's used for airport parking. Its eerie purlieus were employed in the filming of a *Dr Who* episode in 1970. Willowtree Marina and Grand Union Village illustrate where the money is now in canals: not carrying things, but waterside property development.

Map labels

35
1
mp
Town Centre
200
Hayes
Shackles Wharf
Nestle
B
C
E
Tesco
drydock
21 4 21A
3
Bulls Bridge Junction
2
5
mp
201
Grand Junction Arms
park
202
Old Oak Tree
Adelaide Dock
CART
203
The Lamb
37
Bixley Field
mp
A3005 to Southall
A312 to Harrow
A4020 to Uxbridge
20
A4020 to Southall
FF
19
Willowtree Marina (Black Prince)
Tesco
Engineer's Wharf
19 AA
19 AC
19 AD
18
17
17A
17B
38
B455
A40

Key

Key 1
1 site of HMV
2 site of sleeper depot
3 rems of canal depot
4 site of jam factory
5 site of gas works

*Figures refer to main line, allow 1 hour for Paddington Arm between Bulls Bridge (21) and A40 (17B)

PALPABLE - is Pearson's evaluation of the excitement engendered by the Grand Union's descent - through a dozen locks - to the regal Thames; and on the way down the staid waters of the canal are given added impetus by the River Brent, which naturally only adds extra *frisson* to the atmosphere. Indeed, all that is really missing is the canal and its hinterland's more flamboyant past, but we will do what we can to colour that in for you.

Above Norwood Top Lock 90 an arm built in 1913 to serve Otto Monsted's 'Maypole' margarine factory remains in water and used for private moorings. At Three Bridges a road crosses the canal simultaneously as the canal crosses the railway that the Great Western constructed in 1859 to serve its docks at Brentford. It was apparently one of Isambard Kingdom Brunel's last engineering projects and brings to mind a similar sequence of structures - rail over road over river - at Struan on the Highland Railway's main line north of

Blair Atholl. Closely spaced, locks 92-97 were known to working boatmen as the 'Thick of Hanwell'; which was not necessarily a slur on the local populace's intellectual capacity. The locks* (featuring sadly no longer operative side-ponds) are overlooked by the grim facade of a Victorian mental asylum once served by an arched loading bay whose infilled brickwork can still be discerned. The crooner, Al Bowlly, lies buried in a common grave in nearby Hanwell Cemetery, victim of a bomb raid in 1941. The architectural broadcaster and writer, Ian Nairn, is another resident (Plot 22). Below Lock 97 the Brent enters the canal. A worthwhile detour along the Capital Ring will lead you northwards to Wharncliffe Viaduct, Brunel's first substantial engineering challenge out of Paddington.

Between Bridge 205A and Osterley Lock an old sign proudly (if now amusingly) recalls that this length won a pile-driving competition in 1959. Despite being surrounded by urbanisation, the canal has its rural moments, fringed by reed and balsam and shaded by alder and willow.

continued overleaf:

Wharncliffe Viaduct

Hanwell Bridge

Ealing Hospital

The Fox

mp

205A

weir!

Three Bridges

mp

205

Hanwell Locks 92-97
53ft 2ins

70'

206

Boston Manor

weir!

M4

207

mp

Boston Manor House

208

GSK

Brentford FC

Morrisons

Brentford

The Butts

Town Centre

Kew Bridge

Kew Palace

Royal Botanic Gardens

tidal!

Thames Locks 101

Maypole Dock

204

Norwood Locks 90-91
15ft 9ins

203A

1: Trumpers Green Halt
(closed - 1926)

Osterley Lock 98
5ft 7ins

golf course

Osterley Park NT

Piccadilly Line

Clitheroe's Lock 99
7ft 7ins

S mp

209 Gauging Locks 100
5ft 6ins

Syon House

River Thames to Reading

River Thames to London

CART facilities key required to release some of the paddle gear.

continued from page 71:

The M4 motorway and the Piccadilly Line cross the canal/river in quick succession before it bends to encounter Bridge 207, a graceful cast iron structure bearing its place and date of manufacture, Horseley Iron Works near Birmingham 1820. Overlooked by the sky-reflecting headquarters of the pharmaceutical and foodstuffs conglomerate, Glaxo Smith Kline, the navigation passes beneath the Great West Road (which spawned many industrial giants in the 'twenties and 'thirties) followed by the Hounslow Loop of the old London & South Western Railway. As the river veers unnavigably off to the left, the canal broadens into a rectangular basin, still boarded on one side by a cavernous warehouse, partially overhanging the canal and its towpath, reproachfully contrasting with a redevelopment zone of smart apartments (pseudo-romantically known as Heron View and The Island) as if to say 'I am a remnant from a time when this canal worked for its living, you are merely brash upstarts'. Here, moored for up to a fortnight at visitor moorings designated by CART, the more imaginative of boat crews can fantasize that they work for Willow Wren, and that any moment the gaffer - the redoubtable Leslie Morton - will appear on the towpath bearing orders for them to load wheat for Wellingborough or timber for Tipton.

Beyond the moorings, the duplicated (side by side) Gauging Locks are incongruously overlooked by a Holiday Inn, a far cry from the days when Thames lighters would tranship their cargoes into narrowboats in what was once a vibrant dockland setting. Electrically operated (with a CART 'facilities' key) these locks and the following pair of Thames Locks mark the end of the canal's ninety-three mile long journey from Braunston. Boaters proceeding down on to the tidal Thames and upstream towards Reading and beyond are recommended to consult *Pearson's Canal Companion to the Kennet & Avon and River Thames*. Passage of Brentford's Thames Locks is restricted to certain states of the tide and needs to be booked at least 24 hours in advance by telephoning 0208 568 2779. CART publish a Tidal Locks Availability leaflet twice a year which can be found on the internet or obtained from their London office - Tel: 0303 040 4040.

Brentford   Map 37

Redevelopment of Middlesex's old administrative centre marches relentlessly on, yet pockets of old Brentford (such as the charming Butts behind the Market Place, where you will stumble upon a former Boatmen's Institute) remain, establishing a characterful conclusion to your voyage down from the midlands. Gladys Mitchell's 1945 crime novel *The Rising of the Moon* was authentically set in Brentford, whilst devotees of Robert Rankin's literary output will also be in their element.

Eating & Drinking

THE FOX - adjacent foot of Hanwell flight. Tel: 0208 567 4021. *GBG* recommended pub offering London Pride, Doom Bar and Landlord on tap plus guests. Good food and a pretty garden. W7 2PJ
SIRACUSA - Brentford Lock. Tel: 0208 758 0998. Italian overlooking Gauging Locks. TW8 8LF

MAGPIE & CROWN - High Street. Tel: 0208 560 4570. Lively 'dockland' local recommended in the *Good Beer Guide*, notable for its choice of real ales and Continental beers. TW8 8EW
THE WEIR - Market Place. Tel: 0208 568 3600. Sophisticated bar and eating place with a fine garden backing on to the River Brent. Interestingly, the artist Turner stayed here as a boy circa 1785. TW8 8EQ

Shopping

All facilities in High Street, including a Morrisons supermarket at its easterly end.

Things to Do

BOSTON MANOR HOUSE - Boston Manor Road. Tel: 0208 568 2818. Council-owned 17th century mansion open weekends and BHMs, noon-5pm, Apr-Oct. Grounds open throughout year. TW8 9JX
SYON HOUSE - Tel: 0208 560 0881. 17th Century home of the Dukes of Northumberland. TW8 8JG

KEW BRIDGE STEAM MUSEUM - Green Dragon Lane. Tel: 0208 568 4757. Superb museum housed in 19th century waterworks dominated by ornate tower chimney. TW8 0EW
MUSICAL MUSEUM - High Street. Tel: 0208 560 8108. Fascinating collection of mechanical musical machinery from clockwork music boxes to Mighty Wurlitzers. TW8 0DU

Connections

TRAINS - South West Trains services to/from London Waterloo. Tel: 08457 484950.
TUBE - Piccadilly Line services from Boston Manor station into London or out to Heathrow. Tel: 0343 222 1234.
BUSES - alas no No. 667 trolleybuses swishing along the High Street to Hampton Court or Hammersmith now, but access to/from central London by motor omnibus remains an option. Tel: 0871 200 2233.

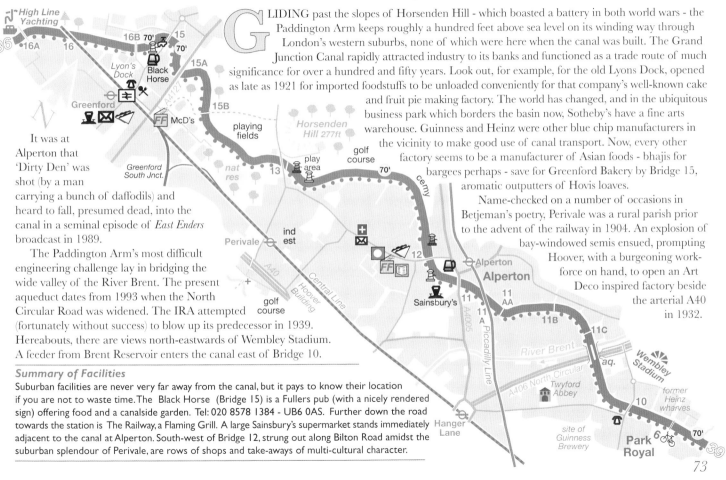

GLIDING past the slopes of Horsenden Hill - which boasted a battery in both world wars - the Paddington Arm keeps roughly a hundred feet above sea level on its winding way through London's western suburbs, none of which were here when the canal was built. The Grand Junction Canal rapidly attracted industry to its banks and functioned as a trade route of much significance for over a hundred and fifty years. Look out, for example, for the old Lyons Dock, opened as late as 1921 for imported foodstuffs to be unloaded conveniently for that company's well-known cake and fruit pie making factory. The world has changed, and in the ubiquitous business park which borders the basin now, Sotheby's have a fine arts warehouse. Guinness and Heinz were other blue chip manufacturers in the vicinity to make good use of canal transport. Now, every other factory seems to be a manufacturer of Asian foods - bhajis for bargees perhaps - save for Greenford Bakery by Bridge 15, aromatic outputters of Hovis loaves.

Name-checked on a number of occasions in Betjeman's poetry, Perivale was a rural parish prior to the advent of the railway in 1904. An explosion of bay-windowed semis ensued, prompting Hoover, with a burgeoning workforce on hand, to open an Art Deco inspired factory beside the arterial A40 in 1932.

It was at Alperton that 'Dirty Den' was shot (by a man carrying a bunch of daffodils) and heard to fall, presumed dead, into the canal in a seminal episode of *East Enders* broadcast in 1989.

The Paddington Arm's most difficult engineering challenge lay in bridging the wide valley of the River Brent. The present aqueduct dates from 1993 when the North Circular Road was widened. The IRA attempted (fortunately without success) to blow up its predecessor in 1939. Hereabouts, there are views north-eastwards of Wembley Stadium. A feeder from Brent Reservoir enters the canal east of Bridge 10.

Summary of Facilities

Suburban facilities are never very far away from the canal, but it pays to know their location if you are not to waste time. The Black Horse (Bridge 15) is a Fullers pub (with a nicely rendered sign) offering food and a canalside garden. Tel: 020 8578 1384 - UB6 0AS. Further down the road towards the station is The Railway, a Flaming Grill. A large Sainsbury's supermarket stands immediately adjacent to the canal at Alperton. South-west of Bridge 12, strung out along Bilton Road amidst the suburban splendour of Perivale, are rows of shops and take-aways of multi-cultural character.

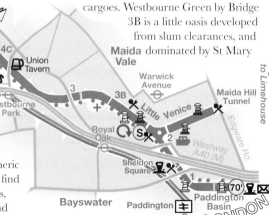

CAN there possibly be a more exciting way of entering the capital? Acton Lane power station, Old Oak Common railway yards, Wormwood Scrubs prison, Kensington gas works and Kensal Green cemetery may, on paper, suggest otherwise, but the reality is a fulminating length of canal which will have even the most sceptical, country-loving canal explorer's adrenalin pumping by the time they reach Ladbrooke Grove. British Waterways, in a last ditch frenzy of indiscriminate bridge-numbering, seemed determined to obfuscate, having you go from 7a to 7b to 7ba to 7d in quick succession, when traditionally they should have been numbered as 6a upwards in reverse order. But such bewilderments only add to the mystique of your progression. Old Oak Wharf, which proclaims that it is 'working towards a canal freight revival', disappointingly appears aspirationally unfulfilled. Contrast that with CrossRail (not to mention HS2), evidence of which is everywhere, and will ultimately transform the landscape.

Bridge 6 ushers Scrub Lane across the canal and, emerging from it, the horizon - redevelopment pending - is filled with the gasometers of Kensington (aka Kensal) gas works. To port, Kensal Green Cemetery replaces the railway yards as the cynosure of your gaze. Many famous people are buried here and a stroll around its atmospheric graves and monuments can prove strangely rewarding. Amongst its permanent residents you'll find the engineers Isambard Kingdom Brunel and Joseph Locke; Victorian novelists Wilkie Collins, William Thackeray and Anthony Trollope; and more recent playwrights Terence Rattigan and

Harold Pinter; plus myriads of more modest 'Murray Poshes' and 'Lupin Pooters'. Opened in 1833, at one time deceased were brought in by boat for burial. There are guided tours on Sundays at 2pm.

Bridges 5 and 5A were side arms into the gasworks. Bridge 4 heralds Ladbroke Grove and Portobello Dock. Refuse was loaded here, destined to fill the old brickworks cavities out Yiewsley and Slough way. Now it's all very chic, and the quirky drinks company, Innocent, have their offices here. On the towpath side by Bridge 4C, a compound contains parked rows of Routemaster double-deckers.

Opened in 1970, the elevated Westway looms out over the canal, its bloated traffic flows moving satisfyingly slower than you are. Modern apartments - not unattractive of their ilk - begin to take advantage of the canal's inherent appeal since it has ceased being a conduit for pungent cargoes. Westbourne Green by Bridge 3B is a little oasis developed from slum clearances, and dominated by St Mary Vale.

Magdalene, a high-spired Victorian church which was employed as a setting in the 1949 film *The Blue Lamp*, debut of Dixon of Dock Green.

It's plausible - if a trifle pat - that Little Venice was so dubbed by Robert Browning, who resided hereabouts. Certainly it's a poetical response to an expanse of water at the meeting of the Paddington Arm and the Regent's Canal. Arboreal, and overlooked by gracious Regency houses, the setting exudes exceptional charm. Residential moorings provide the opportunity to enjoy an enviable amphibious lifestyle in central London, whilst the canal setting attracts large numbers of visitors who perhaps subconsciously perceive the canal as a potential escape route from the pressures of everyday urban existence, even if they get no further than

a trip-boat voyage to Camden Lock.

Framed by Maida Avenue and Blomfield Road (where the novelist and early IWA secretary, Elizabeth Jane Howard, once lived) the Regent's Canal leaves Little Venice via the shadowy portal of Maida Hill Tunnel on its way to meet the Thames at Limehouse, a fascinating route which lack of space decrees are left to Pearsonless devices for the time being, though we have aspirations of covering it in the next edition by dint of some gentle shunting. The Paddington Arm, on the other hand, makes a dog-leg turn into its wide terminal basin, redeveloped to good effect with some excellent visitor moorings provided in the shadow of St Mary's famous hospital and all those Welsh, rugby-playing interns.

Paddington

As a launchpad for London, Paddington could hardly be bettered. Eschew the obvious, embrace the esoteric. Aldgate, Bloomsbury and Clerkenwell are the offbeat bits of the capital you should make it your business to see, as opposed to the Palace, Tower and Tussauds. The world - if you'll pardon the pun - is your Oyster Card.

Eating & Drinking
ABERDEEN STEAK HOUSE - Praed Street. Tel: 0207 420 6200. Retro food for hungry boaters. Praed (rhymes with paid) Street derives its name from William Praed, Chairman of the Grand Junction Canal Co. W2 1RH
THE BRIDGE HOUSE - Westbourne Terrace Road. Tel: 0207 266 4326. Comfortable pub adjacent Little Venice and adjoining Canal Cafe Theatre. W2 6NG
LA VILLE - Edgware Road. Tel: 0207 706 2620. Charming Italian cafe/restaurant perched over the western portal of Maida Hill Tunnel. W2 1HT
SUMMERHOUSE - canalside, Blomfield Road, Little Venice. Tel: 0207 286 6752. Eat well and watch the boats go by. W9 2PD

Paddington Basin

UNION TAVERN - Woodfield Road (canalside bridge 4C). Tel: 0207 286 1886. This *Good Beer Guide* listed pub makes for a nice easy stroll out from Little Venice. They specialise in London and Home Counties real ales and provide excellent food. On warm days you can eat and drink al fresco on a rooftop patio overlooking the Grand Union. W2 2BA
WATERSIDE CAFE - Little Venice. Tel: 0207 266 1066. Breakfasts (from 9am), light lunches and teas on board this cafe boat or at adjoining towpath tables. CART cards and keys on sale. W2 6NE

Shopping
There's a Sainsbury's 'local' in Sheldon Square, whilst a Tesco Express and post office can be found at the furthest end of Paddington Basin. Otherwise you'll have to hoof it to Harrods or Fortnum & Mason!

Things to Do
'When a man is tired of London, he is tired of life'.

Connections
TRAINS - First Great Western services out of Paddington to Hayes & Harlington provide a useful resource for walks along the Paddington Arm. Tel: 08457 484950.

Laughton Hills

Leicester Line

SILLITOE'S early story springs to mind, retitled *The Loneliness of the Long Distance Boater*, as you assuredly come to terms with the Leicester Section's remote atmosphere. Canal, railway, and two generations of main road attempt to squeeze simultaneously through a gap in the hills between the villages of Ashby St Ledgers and Watford. By now you will be beginning to realise that you get nowhere fast on this stretch of canal, but as there isn't anywhere particular to go, this barely seems to matter. The bridge which carries the West Coast Main Line over the canal repays a second glance, being curiously constructed with barrel vaulting at ninety degrees to the waterway rather than the forty-five degree angle suggested by the configuration of the railway. Presumably it was Robert Stephenson's work, the classical decoration of the ironwork girders and railings certainly bears his hallmark. Watford Gap motorway services are redolent of an altogether different era of transport. When it opened in 1959, it was the forerunner of the kind of establishment most of us have grown to loathe. In the Sixties and Seventies many famous pop groups called in here on their way back from gigs in the small hours of the night.

Boats coagulate at Watford Locks like parties of ramblers queuing to climb a stile. Happily you are no longer expected to fathom their complex operation - which ran to three pages of text in the early British Waterways guides - rather you are encouraged to make yourself known to the lock-keeper, whereafter he or she will be only too happy to guide you through the flight's arcane and esoteric machinations.

Watford Locks raise the canal to its summit level of 412 feet. At the turn of the century there were plans to replace the flight with an inclined plane like that at Foxton, but the scheme was shelved. When the Grand Union was formed in 1929 there were further proposals for the flight to be widened, but these also languished. Crick Tunnel is almost a mile long and, in common with the other two tunnels on the route, doesn't have a towpath. In the old days boat horses found their way over the top via Watford Road and Boathorse Lane, the way that walkers have still to trudge today.

Watford

A pretty estate village which has somehow survived the building of the M1 past its back door. There's no shop, but in extremis you can find your way surreptitiously from Bridge 6 to the adjacent motorway services.

Crick

Useful watering-hole on the Rugby-Northampton road. Post office stores adjacent to Bridge 12, Co-op with cash machine deeper into the village, and there's a garden centre beside the marina. Three pubs in the centre, but the closest establishment to the canal is The Moorings, a comfortable canalside cafe/restaurant open daily from 10am (ex Mon, and Sun eves). Tel: 01788 822517 - NN6 7SQ. Stagecoach bus service 96 runs to Rugby and Northampton. Tel: 0871 200 2233.

THE A14 attempts to shatter the inherent calm of the Leicester Section, but its brutality is transitory, and on either side the canal continues to negotiate its narrow, shallow, back of beyond summit. Moor hereabouts for the night and there are hardly any lights in the landscape. Such a feeling of loneliness is engendered that you feel compelled to wave to tractor drivers in distant fields or soliloquise with the cattle who stoop to drink in the reedy margins of the cut. In a sense you are seeing the countryside as our forefathers did, before the motor car gave us a spurious familiarity with distance. The scenery is a homespun tweed of wooded hilltops and distant church spires; hunting country personified. Though they are now predominantly sheep grazed or turned over to crops, the fields still bear patterns of ridge & furrow. Beacon-topped Crack's Hill is a glacial moraine. Footpaths render the summit easily reachable and indentification of the panoramic views on offer is aided by a topograph. There are proposals to erect a stone circle on the hill.

Yelvertoft

Well removed from the nearest main road - its railway station, when it had one, lay two miles to the north - Yelvertoft is arguably the pleasantest village on this part of the Leicester Section, and being built almost entirely of rich red coloured local brick, is typical of its ilk. Moorings are to be had between bridges 19 and 20, but avoid the sharp bends! Facilities include a small post office store and Alex Chambers' splendid, Italian inspired deli/butchers, Squ!sito, open daily ex Mon & Tue - Tel: 01788 824123 - ready meals delivered to your boat! Bus 96 to Rugby & Northampton daily ex Suns. The Knightley Arms is an unassuming village local. Tel: 01788 823555 - NN6 6LF

This part of the Leicester Section's towpath tends to be narrow: comfortable enough for single file walking but hardly conducive for happy cycling. Sections coincide with the Jurassic Way which connects Stamford to Banbury. Beware protruding pilings underfoot. Adopt 'goose step'.

Garden Centre

40

14
mp 36
15
70'
16
13
Crick Marina
Crack's Hill
mp 35
17
by-road to Rugby
Yelvertoft
18
Yelvertoft Marina
Flint Hill Farm
19
Yelvertoft Wharf
mp 34
21
20
22
Heygates
mp 33
23
Winwick Grange
24
25
Winwick Manor
26
mp 32
27
spill-weir
A14 to M1 Jnct. 19
Park Farm
32
mp 29
31
Jurassic Way
33
42
Winwick
mp 31
28
29A
29
70'
30
mp 30
A14 to Kettering
Hemplow Hills

TRAVERSING its rural summit, the 'Old' Grand Union crosses the infant Avon which forms the boundary between Northamptonshire and Leicestershire. Excluding the Thames, this Avon has probably had more written about it than any other English river. Yet here, trickling beneath the canal embankment, it looks modest enough; and one suspects that had it not been for the influence of a certain W. Shakespeare (and oddly enough it's difficult to see where, if at all, the Avon is mentioned in his works) the river wouldn't have collected the plaudits that it has.

In the distance the Avon widens to form Stanford Reservoir which supplies drinking water to Rugby. In the foreground runs the trackbed of the London & North Western Railway's Rugby to Peterborough line. How pleasant it would be to see a local train again, weaving grey ribbons of smoke and steam across the countryside, pausing momentarily at remote stations, miles from the villages they purported to serve. Branch lines such as this knitted England's landscape together; defined its diversity; and when they were dismantled part of the fabric of rural society was irrevocably torn asunder. But magically the canal survives, albeit concerned with tourism rather than trade. Signs of the latter can be discerned by Bridge 40 where a widening of water and a ruined jetty mark the site of a wharf at which locally dug gravel was loaded on to boats.

Another wharf was situated at North Kilworth. Wharfingering here was kept in the Woodhouse family who were also landlords of the long defunct inn as well as operators of a small fleet of boats engaged in bringing coal in from Derbyshire and Warwickshire collieries for domestic use, and lime for local agriculture. Apparently,

continued on page 82:

'Harborough Arm'

Watford Locks

Bridge 2

Welford Wharf

Bridge 32

Leicester
Line Cameos

Foxton

Market Harborough Basin 1

Market Harborough Basin 2

Crick Tunnel

Foxton Locks

Welford Arm

81

continued from page 79:

one of the Woodhouse boats was contracted to carry scrap when the inclined plane at Foxton was being demolished, but its back was broken under the weight of the load and it sank at the foot of the flight. L.T.C. Rolt mentioned the family's pub in *Narrow Boat*. North of the wharf the canal winds through a deep, tree-bowered cutting to the portal of Husbands Bosworth Tunnel.

The Welford Arm

Not so much an arm, more a finger, this branch was dug to bring water from Welford, Sulby and Naseby reservoirs to feed the main line. But a certain amount of trade developed in limestone and bricks, whilst coal was still being brought to Welford by boat at the end of the Second World War. Thereafter the arm fell into decay - though retaining its role as a feeder - and was allowed to silt up. It remained unnavigable for twenty years until its re-opening in 1969.

Leaving the main line, the arm establishes its individuality by dint of its overbridges being numbered from one upwards. The adjacent ridges close in to create a feeling of intimacy. After a mile the arm rises through a diminutive lock to reach the highest pound on the whole of the former Grand Union system. The terminus is just around the corner, and the arm's deceptive calm is exposed as an illusion by the density of boats moored in two lagoons. Remnants of the limekilns which once brought trade to the arm can be seen, and there are several interesting waymarked walks to be had in the vicinity. A detour up the Welford Arm is difficult to resist. Boaters are, by definition, explorers at heart, and the end of the arm makes a pleasant overnight mooring with the facilities of the village and the wildlife of the reservoirs near at hand.

The country writer 'BB' (alias Denys Watkins-Pitchford, who illustrated *Narrow Boat*) included several passages describing the flora and fauna of the Welford Arm in his book *The Wayfaring Tree*. He lived at Shrubland House in Welford after his marriage in 1939. Boaters are well advised to turn at the winding hole and drop back on to the visitor moorings, as the end of the arm tends to fill up with boats.

Welford   Map 42

Welford straddles the old A50 (now A5199), a road which wandered its way from Northampton to Warrington via Leicester and Stoke-on-Trent, encountering a fair few canals en route. Handsome ironstone church and many attractive vernacular houses, characteristically of redbrick and, in some instances, thatch. Shakespeare's Avon Way leads to Naseby, scene, in 1645, of the decisive battle of the Civil War. Nearer at hand a public footpath bisects the canal feeder reservoirs of Welford and Sulby.

Eating & Drinking

WHARF INN - canalside at terminus. Tel: 01858 575075. Contemporaneous with the opening of the arm in 1814, this stuccoed and castellated pub is open from noon daily. Spacious garden alongside the strippling Avon. NN6 6JQ

ELEVENSES - High Street. Tel: 01858 575505. Teas, coffees and gifts. NN6 6HT

Shopping

Post office stores on High Street.

Connections

BUSES - service 60 provides infrequent links with M Harborough and Northampton. Tel: 0871 200 2233.

North Kilworth   Map 42

There are too many lorries using the main road to make the walk into North Kilworth pleasurable for those off the canal - even though it boasts a pavement. The story goes that a Kilworth woman - whose German husband was interned during the Second World War - had her Alsatian dog shot by the village policeman simply because it was a *German* Shepherd. Kilworth House is a country house hotel with an outdoor theatre.

Husbands Bosworth   Map 43

Husbands Bosworth acquired its prefix in the 17th century in deference to Market Bosworth, twenty miles to the north-west. The other notable event of the period concerned the execution in 1616 of nine local 'witches' for allegedly causing fits in the grandson of the Lord of the Manor. Six further 'witches' were similarly accused but pardoned by James I. Fast forward three centuries and HB had a WWII aerodrome built on its doorstep, a facility now used by gliders. It is a sizeable village of winding lanes (one enchantingly called Honeypot) embracing predominantly brick houses of much charm. Limited (and somewhat shallow) mooring space is available by Bridge 46. Facilities include The Bell Inn (Tel: 01858 880246 - LE17 6JZ), a sandwich bar/cafe called Catering Corner, and post office stores. Bus service 58 runs bi-hourly Mon-Sat to Market Harborough and Lutterworth - Tel: 0871 200 2233.

43 GU LEICESTER SECTION Husbands Bosworth 5mls/0lks/1.5hrs

PIERCING the watershed, Husbands Bosworth Tunnel ushers you effectively from one side of England to the other. Down there in the valley runs the River Welland which, like many of life's insuperable difficulties, eventually comes out in The Wash. Pedestrians have to walk over the top of Husbands Bosworth Tunnel, but it is a thoroughly enjoyable detour encountering, en route, a graceful occupation bridge across the grassy trackbed of the dismantled railway. The bosky, musky horse-path can get a little overgrown during the summer months - though nothing that the long-suffering country walker isn't already resigned emotionally to deal with. Elsewhere the towpath - framed

by a shade-providing hedge of considerable height - is fine for single-file pedestrians, but protruding roots and pockets of erosion render cycling out of the question. The landscape is gorgeously typical of The Shires, consisting of broad, high hedged pastures interspersed with fox coverts, spinneys and substantial houses erected as hunting lodges by the fox and hounds brigade. One such is Lubenham Lodge, adjacent to Bridge 58. Sheltered by tall pines and chestnuts, the property evokes a

sense of timeless, gracious living and well-being. Its dormer windows must offer a peerless prospect over the Vale. Not to be outdone, the eponymous house on the neighbouring hillside was built to the design of the Arts & Crafts architect, Charles Voysey.

Just as - in the words of the old song - the mountains of Mourne sweep down to the sea, so do the Laughton Hills sweep luxuriantly down to the Leicester Section of the Grand Union Canal. A paltry five hundred or so feet above sea level, in the context of the gentle Welland Valley, the hills appear of much greater significance along a canal which clings to the 412ft contour. Sheep and cattle graze the slopes and buzzards call overhead. Mile after ravishing mile the countryside unrolls its beauty for the benefit of the canal traveller, invoking a sense of well-being whatever the weather. Solely mileposts and bridge numbers register movement, otherwise you could be forgiven for thinking that you are in some extraordinary sort of trance. Grand Union (nee Junction, hence the 'J') mileposts measure the distance to and from Leicester. Fascinatingly, the 'Old' Grand Union used trees as 'living' mileposts. In the 1980s the OUCS replanted these, measuring the miles to and from Foxton.

LEICESTERSHIRE folk appear to regard Foxton Locks as their own personal street-theatre. They descend on the flight in droves. Abandoning their vehicles to the car parks, they visit the pubs, they board the trip boats, they marvel at the remains of the inclined plane, they mill about, giving scant rein to their children's excitement, much to the chagrin of the lock-keepers who live with perpetual fear of tragedy. The inland navigator plays a walk-on part in Foxton's soap opera, and is expected to respond cheerfully to bizarre questions and fatuous remarks with the amused tolerance of a Gulliver amidst Lilliputians.

That Foxton is a canal centre at all is due to historical accident. The original concept, dating from 1793, was for a canal to link Leicester with Northampton; connection southwards with the Grand Junction Canal would be made at the latter town. In the event, the Leicestershire & Northamptonshire Union Canal - built to broadbeam dimensions - ran out of capital and was forced to terminate for a dozen ignominious years at the village of

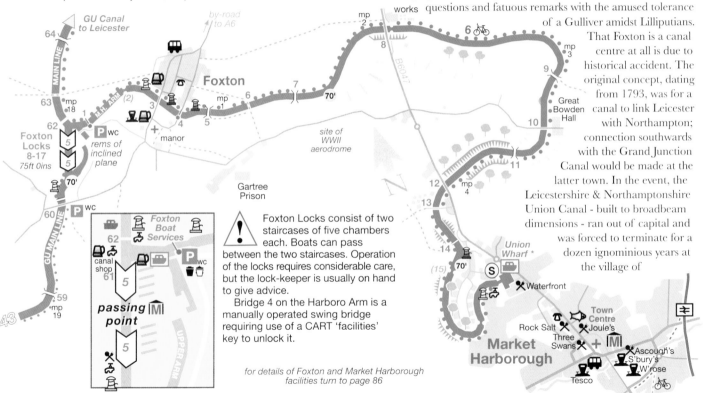

Foxton Locks consist of two staircases of five chambers each. Boats can pass between the two staircases. Operation of the locks requires considerable care, but the lock-keeper is usually on hand to give advice.

Bridge 4 on the Harboro Arm is a manually operated swing bridge requiring use of a CART 'facilities' key to unlock it.

for details of Foxton and Market Harborough facilities turn to page 86

* ABC Boat Hire/Tillerman/Canal Boat Club

Debdale a mile or so north of Foxton. Progress southwards as far as Market Harborough was completed in 1809, but the direct route to Northampton was never built. In exasperation, a new company was promoted to link the Leics & Northants with the Grand Junction. Known as the 'Grand Union', it charted a 23-mile route from Norton to Foxton including two precipitous flights of narrowbeam locks at either end of the twenty mile summit.

Thus the seeds were sown for Foxton's prominence. The village that had never been earmarked as a junction settled down to three-quarters of a century of fluctuating trade. The 'Grand Union' never made much profit and was bought out by the Grand Junction in 1894. Fellows, Morton & Clayton, the route's prime users, were by this time agitating for improvements to the bottle-neck staircases at Watford and Foxton and for a widening of the gauge. In what, with hindsight, can be seen as an over-enthusiastic response, the Grand Junction proposed boat lifts, or more properly, inclined planes, at both sites. Only the one at Foxton was built, it opened in 1900. Archive photographs reveal the astonishing grandeur of the inclined plane: an upper and lower dock, separated by a 1:4 gradient laid with rails, supporting two counterbalanced tanks each capable of taking a barge or pair of narrowboats.

But for all their tub-thumping, FMC's trade never built to a level commensurate with the viable operation of the lift. Days were wont to go by when the attendants had nothing better to do than stoke the boiler and squirt oil on the moving parts: the railways had long since cornered the bulk of traffic between the East Midlands and London. Paradoxically, FMC and other carriers were irked that the lift was closed at night, occasioning delay to the 24 hour 'fly' boats which used the route. In response, the locks - unused since the opening of the lift - were reinstated and, inevitably, it was not long before these were deemed economically preferable to the lift, closure of which is recorded as having taken place in November 1910. The structure lay derelict through the years of the First World War, but was demolished in 1928 by a firm of Shropshire scrap merchants, who paid a paltry £250 for the privilege. The Foxton Inclined Plane Trust have ambitious proposals to restore the planc to full working order.

The Market Harborough Arm

The scheme for a through route to Northampton moribund, the canal between Foxton and Market Harborough lapsed into branch status, a character prevalent to this day. Busier since a hire base was established in the revitalised terminal basin, the arm still tends to attract the sort of boaters who are never happier than when poking their inquisitive prows up the lonely backwaters of the system. The arm circles the skirts of Gallows Hill. To the north-east there are splendid vistas across the village-sprinkled valley of the River Welland. During the Second World War they built a bomber base on the top of Gallow Hill on a site now occupied by Gartree Prison, a maximum security establishment whose high walls and floodlights can occasionally be glimpsed from the canal. Some years ago a prisoner made a daring escape up a rope ladder dangling from a helicopter flown over the prison compound by an accomplice.

By Bridge 8 there is a 'rendering' plant, a euphemistic term for the disposal of animal parts. Locals have likened the cloying aroma to rotting meat broth. Fortunately, you're just passing. Otherwise, the arm is largely undisturbed and undemonstrative, fringed with reeds, arrowhead and water lilies, its narrow channel measured, mile by mile, with the aid of simple iron mileposts counting the distance from Foxton.

Boxing the compass, the arm's entrance into Market Harborough is abruptly suburban - all lawns, laurels and lachrymose willows. The terminal basin looks exemplary these days, though it seems unfair that visiting boaters have to moor outside its historic confines unless they ask at the boatyard and pay a small fee. After all, this was the scene in 1950 of the fledgling Inland Waterways Association's first festival. It proved a resounding success, even though the Association was being torn apart by a deep schism between its two chief founders, Robert Aickman and Tom Rolt. Over a hundred boats attended and fifty thousand visitors enjoyed the festival's mixture of canal exhibits and theatrical entertainment. One imagines that the whole event would have made a marvellous film subject for an Ealing Comedy. Perhaps the ghosts of Rolt and Aickman, still at loggerheads, will disturb your sleep with their bickering.

Foxton

Map 44

Foxton village basks in the sun like a sleek cat that has just had two helpings of cream. Property prices here must average six figures, and on weekdays when the bread-winners are away it is as quiet as a nunnery. Up on their hilltop, the manor and the church daydream of a feudal past.

Eating & Drinking

FOXTON LOCKS INN - canalside bottom lock. Tel: 0116 279 1515. Popular refurbished 'all-day' pub overlooking the foot of the locks. Wide range of catering. LE16 7RA

BRIDGE 61 - bottom lock. Tel: 0116 279 2285. Cosy antidote to Foxton Locks Inn. Food and locally-brewed Langton ales. LE16 7RA

BLACK HORSE - adjacent Bridge 3 (uphill). Tel: 01858 545250. Comfortable Greene King pub with conservatory restaurant and lovely garden overlooked by village church. LE16 7RD

SHOULDER OF MUTTON - adjacent Bridge 3 (downhill). Tel: 01858 545964. Pub with Chinese restaurant and accommodation. LE16 7RB
There are cafes at the top and bottom of the locks pandering to the busy traffic in gongoozlers.

Shopping

RURAL TRADING - Main Street (Black Horse). Enterprising venture which brings a general store back to the village after many years absence. Fresh foods, fruit and vegetables, dairy produce, provisions, toiletries, newspapers etc. Open from 9am-5pm Mon-Sat, 9.30am-2pm Sun.
Laundry facilities are available from Foxton Boat Services.

Things to Do

THE BOILER HOUSE - refurbished museum devoted to the inclined plane. Open daily in summer, weekends in winter. Entry charge. Tel: 0116 279 2657. LE16 7RA

Connections

BUSES - Centrebus 44 operates approximately hourly to/from Market Harbough Mon-Sat. Tel: 0871 200 2233.

Market Harborough

Map 44

Watered by the River Welland, Market Harborough is an inherently good looking town, exuding a healthy vitality without being too self-consciously touristy. In any case, one welcomes some degree of hustle and bustle as a palliative to the soporific charm of the Leicester Section. Here and there stand some charming architectural oddities. Take, for example, Church Square, dominated by the parish church of St Dionysius with its soaring ashlar spire and sundial bearing the admirable motto "Improve the Time". This is also the location of a wonderfully picturesque timber building on stilts that was formerly the grammar school. You can sit beside it on a bench commemorating Jack Gardner, British Heavyweight Champion 1950-2. Nearby, a handsome textile mill (Symington's corset factory) looks as though it has surreptitiously been spirited down the A6 from Stockport on a Pickford's low-loader. In fact there are two strands to the Symington family, Scots brothers who arrived in the town in 1827. James Symington married a stay-maker and never looked back - in their 20th century heyday Symingtons were innovators of the Liberty Bodice. William Symington turned his talents to food production and the company's name became synonymous with pea soup and table cream.

Eating & Drinking

THE WATERFRONT - Union Wharf. Tel: 01858 434702. Restaurant & bar located in the former Terminal Warehouse with tables spilling out on to the quayside itself in the summer months. LE16 7UW

ASCOUGH'S - St Mary's Road. Tel: 01858 466966. Highly regarded restaurant (previously on High St.) open for lunch and dinner Tue-Sat. LE16 7DU

JOULE'S EATING HOUSE - off High Street. Tel: 01858 463250. Blissfully eccentric establishment additionally offering collectables and a laundry service! LE16 7AF

THE THREE SWANS - High Street. Tel: 01858 466644. Refurbished Best Western hotel once famous for belonging to the eccentric inn-keeper John Fothergill who wrote about it in his book *My Three Inns*. Also referred to by Aickman in his description of the first National Rally in *The River Runs Uphill*. Bar and restaurant meals and a wrought-iron sign depicting the three swans hanging over the High Street. LE16 7NJ

ROCK SALT - High Street. Tel: 01858 462963. Stylish seafood restaurant and grill housed in what was formerly Ascough's (see above) open for lunch and dinner daily except for Sundays. LE16 7NL

Shopping

There are Sainsbury's, Tesco and Waitrose supermarkets. The market hall operates on Tuesdays, Fridays and Saturdays and there's a Farmer's Market held in the Square on the first Thursday in the month. Elsewhere, there are some charmingly individual retailers like Bates the butcher, Hobbs the fishmonger, Duncan Murray the wine merchants, and Emerson & Wests, caterers since 1886. Bookshop called Quinns in the same alley as Joule's Eating House (also two secondhand dealers).

Things to Do

HARBOROUGH MUSEUM - Adam & Eve Street. Tel: 0116 305 3627. Excellent town museum housed in former corset factory. Open Tue-Sat. LE16 7AG

Connections

TRAINS - East Midlands to/from London & Leicester etc. Tel: 08457 484950.

BUSES - services 44 (Foxton) and 58 (Husbands Bosworth) provide useful Mon-Sat links for towpathers Tel: 0871 200 2233.

TAXIS - Central Cabs. Tel: 01858 461451.

Kelmscott

Upper Thames

45 RIVER THAMES Lechlade 2mls/11k/0.5hrs

TURNING on his heel, and setting off across the meadows for the town of Lechlade, Ernest Temple Thurston looked back just once to see that Eynsham Harry had hitched Fanny the boat horse back to the *Flower of Gloster's* tow line before embarking on its return trip along the Thames & Severn Canal. That was 1910 and, for the present at least, Eynsham Harry's journey cannot be replicated, though the Cotswolds Canal Trust have aspirations of eventually returning that most comely of canals to navigation. Temple Thurston's footprints, however, can be followed, albeit briefly. And if one imagines that he would have viewed the impedimenta of interpretive boards and picnic tables with something approaching scorn, and that he departed Lechlade on a train for Oxford - a simple arrangement of civilisation beyond us now - it is a nonetheless pleasing fancy to re-enact those inital steps from Inglesham at the outset of your exploration of the Upper Thames.

Many a 'small hour' was spent agonising over how to approach our coverage of the Upper Thames. Our natural inclination would have been to begin - as most boaters do - at the Oxford end. It generally makes more sense, though, to follow a river downstream; to go, as it were, with the flow. And because the *Kennet & Avon and River Thames Canal Companion* complies with this conceit, it seemed best to follow suit, even if accompanied on our researches by more than the odd qualm or two. Pearson's users are however - by and large - an intelligent bunch, owing more to Paul Theroux's wisdom-filled definition of travellers (who: 'don't know where they're going') than tourists (who: 'don't know where they've been'), and will be quite adept at following the maps in either direction.

So let's commence our description of the lovely Upper Thames at Inglesham, where the Waterway Recovery Group are painstakingly restoring the lock, and where one of the Thames & Severn Canal's characteristic round-houses can be seen to good effect from across the river. Also at Inglesham - on the Wiltshire bank of the Thames - stands the 13th century church of St John the Baptist which boasts a

Saxon carving of the Madonna and child. Cared for now by the Churches Conservation Trust, St John's was previously saved from decay by none other than William Morris.

As befits the largest - indeed the *only* - town on the upper reaches, Lechlade (jostled by the counties of Gloucestershire, Wiltshire and Oxfordshire - and formerly Berkshire) has been shaped, commercially and culturally by the presence of the Thames on its doorstep. Today a marina provides boating activity where once stone and cheese and wool were the prevalent cargoes. Lechlade or Halfpenny Bridge dates from 1793, its colloquial name derived from the toll paid by pedestrians (unless they could convince the toll-keeper that they were bound for the church!) until 1839. Downstream the Thames essays a charming course overlooked by the soaring Perpendicular spire of St Lawrence,

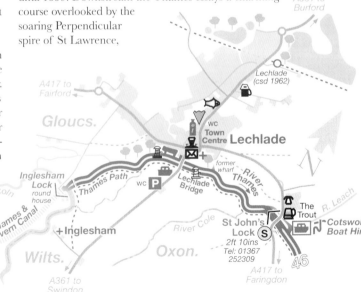

together with a number of gracious private gardens, some sporting elegant gazebos. Informal public moorings are available on the south, Wiltshire bank of the river against a wide expanse of watermeadows.

St John's Lock is the highest on the Thames, but if you travel all the way to Teddington you will arguably be unable to find one better tended. It is graced by a reclining statue of Father Thames, postcards of which are obtainable from the lock-keeper. It is the work of R. Monti and was sculpted for the Crystal Palace in 1854. Between 1958 and 1974 it stood by the source of the Thames at Thames Head, but was prone to the attention of vandals, and this lockside was considered a safer spot for

the old man's contemplation of his river.

Downstream of the lock cut two Thames tributaries join the channel: the River Cole, from the south flows off the Marlborough Downs below Swindon and forms the boundary between Wiltshire and Oxfordshire; the River Leach rises high up on the Cotswolds, lends its name to the Fosse Way village of Northleach, and travels fifteen miles to meet the Thames - once it was said to yield 'the finest watercress in England' which was loaded on to a train each evening at Lechlade station for transit to Covent Garden. Lechlade falls astern and the Thames begins to make it obvious that it would prefer to be alone.

Lechlade
Map 45

What's not to like about Lechlade? It would be difficult to manufacture a more amenable town to accompany the head of navigation on the River Thames. Formerly at the meeting place of four counties, Lechlade graces the south-eastern corner of Gloucestershire with thoroughfares of mellow 'Cotswold' stone. Shelley wrote a poem about St Lawrence's in 1815 (having rowed all the way from old Windsor!) and its gargoyles are remarkable!

Eating & Drinking
COLLEYS - High Street. Tel: 01367 252218. Highly regarded brasserie style restaurant. Lunch Tue-Sun, dinner Tue-Sat. GL7 3AE
CROWN INN - High Street. Tel: 01367 252198. Pub with its own Halfpenny Brewery. GL7 3AE
KHUSI - Burford Street. Tel: 01367 252956. Indian restaurant open daily from noon. GL7 3AP
MONICA'S PLAICE - High Street. Tel: 01367 250050. Eat in or take-away fish & chips. GL7 3AE
OLD SWAN INN - Burford Street. Tel: 01367 253571. Comfortably refurbished inn. GL7 3AP
LYNWOOD & CO - Market Square. Tel: 01367 253707. Nicely appointed cafe. GL7 3AB

Lechlade (or Halfpenny) Bridge

L'ARTIGIANO - High Street. Tel: 01367 252373. Italian restaurant open daily (ex Mondays) for lunch/dinner. GL7 3AD
RIVERSIDE INN - Tel: 01367 252534. Arkells pub offering food and accommodation. GL7 3AQ
TROUT INN - Faringdon Road. Tel: 01367 252313. One of three 'Trouts' beside the Upper Thames. Bar and restaurant meals, nice big garden, customer moorings. GL7 3HA

Shopping
Highlights include Cutler & Bayliss butcher/greengrocer/deli and Vin Est wine merchants, both on Burford Street. A Londis

convenience store is located in the Market Square and provides most day to day necessities. There's also a pharmacy, pet shop, post office, and Barclays bank with cash machine. Several antique, craft and gift shops provide counterpoint to day to day requirements, notably a shop selling Christmas goods, *all year round*.

Things to Do
BOATING - Lechlade Angling (Tel: 0790 015 4098) and Cotswold Boat Hire (Tel: 01793 727083/0794 799 3784) offer various types of craft for informal day hire. The Cotswold Canals Trust operate a launch called *Inglesham* at weekends and Bank holidays on a half hour round trip from Lechlade to the entrance to the Thames & Severn Canal - Tel: 0778 748 5294.

Connections
BUSES - there is *no* direct link to Oxford! Services 74/77 run to/from Swindon and Cirencester, but of most use to Thames Path walkers is service 64 which operates five times per day (but *not* Suns!) to Carterton where you can change for Bampton and Oxford. Tel: 0871 200 2233.
TAXIS - CT's. Tel: 01367 252575.

OCCASIONALLY, in its inexperience, this youthfully navigable Thames coils itself up like a mischievous hose pipe, producing fiendishly difficult bends for the steerers of anything longer than a cabin cruiser to deal with. From the relative safety of the Thames Path, ramblers can watch the less-adept's attempts to extract themselves from sandbanks with feigned concern and hidden glee: it was always thus. But whether walking or boating, or simply picnicking on its banks, there is no escaping the inherent beauty of the river, nor its capacity for filtering out the less admirable excesses of 21st century living.

Parcels of land at Buscot are within the care of the National Trust. The riverside parsonage can be visited, though only by prior appointment. Its car park occupies the site of a wharf where, amongst other items, local cheese was despatched by barge to Oxford and London. Buscot church boasts some fine 19th century stained glass by Burne-Jones and has associations with the Brotherhood of the Way. It lies close to the river on what used to be its Berkshire bank, but foliage hides it away throughout the summer months. The churchyard contains the unmarked grave of Florence Bravo who was embroiled in one of the great unsolved crimes of the Victorian era. She was suspected of poisoning her second husband, but nothing could be proven. It hardly mattered, she died prematurely from alcohol abuse. Her father was Robert Campbell, a Scottish engineer who'd made a fortune in the Australian goldfields. Having acquired the Buscot estate, he set out to revolutionise agriculture in the area by growing sugar beet, processed - at a long vanished distillery near the lock - into alcohol spirit, exported to France for brandy making. A network of narrow gauge railway lines spread across the district to facilitate transport. A gas works was built, and a brick and tile works erected with a wharf at the end of a short canal off the main river channel. A reservoir was dug to improve irrigation, pumps being driven by a huge waterwheel located beside the lock. Campbell was an enlightened employer who restricted his workforce (which included a number of Frenchmen hired for their inside knowledge of the brandy industry) to a nine hour day. All this model endeavour came to an abrupt halt in the financial crash which followed the Crimean War, and what with the scandal surrounding his daughter, Campbell went to an early (but headstoned) grave in neighbouring Eaton Hastings.

Eaton Footbridge marks the site of the last flash lock on the river, extant until as recently (in the full course of river time) as 1937. It was operated by an arcane arrangement of 'rymers' and 'paddles' which is now to be seen only (on the weir channel) at Northmoor Lock (Map 50). A pub called

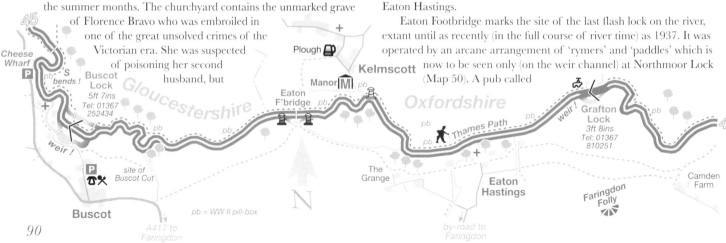

Cheese Wharf
P

Buscot Lock
5ft 7ins
Tel: 01367
252434

weir !

Gloucestershire

'S bends !'

pb

P

site of Buscot Cut

Buscot

A417 to Faringdon

pb = WW II pill-box

N

Plough

Kelmscott

Manor M

Eaton F'bridge

Oxfordshire

Thames Path

pb

pb

The Grange

Eaton Hastings

by-road to Faringdon

weir !

Grafton Lock
3ft 8ins
Tel: 01367
810251

pb

Faringdon Folly

Camden Farm

The Anchor overlooked the river here until it burnt down with loss of life in 1979. But it is perhaps Kelmscott Manor which is the cynosure on the reach between the locks at Buscot and Grafton. Sixteenth century in origin, with its mellow stonework masked from the river by a raucous high-rise community of rooks, it is inevitably for its associations with William Morris and the Pre-Raphaelites that the house is valued now. Morris arrived here in 1871, initially sharing the manor with Dante Gabriel Rossetti who paid rather too much attention to Jane Morris (who sat for many of his best known paintings) for the household's equilibrium. Morris was a man of tremendous energy - political activist, forward thinker, designer of wallpapers, stained glass windows and furniture (though *not* of motor cars) early supporter of the Arts & Crafts movement, founder of the Society for the Protection of Ancient Buildings, and writer of poetry and prose - and he employed

Kelmscott as a summer retreat for a quarter of a century and relished in particular its proximity to the Thames, alongside which his busy workaday life was spent at Hammersmith. His Utopian work of fiction, *News From Nowhere*, describes a dream-voyage upstream from London to Kelmscott, encountering above Oxford 'whispering beds of reeds and willows dipping into the stream'. He must, presumably lie most contentedly in St George's churchyard alongside his wife Jane and daughters Jenny and May.

Grafton Lock is timelessly remote, having about it the air of one of those small country stations of yore. In this low-lying district, Faringdon Hill (aka Folly) is a prominent landmark some three miles south of the river. The slender tower which tops it was erected at the behest of the eccentric Lord Berners in 1935.

Buscot   Map 46
A model settlement dating from 1879, thankfully unimpinged upon by the A417, though you will have to brave its verges should you wish to visit the National Trust's Buscot Park, a mile south-east of the river: Tel: 01367 240932 - SN7 8BU. The Old Parsonage is also a NT property, though only accessible by written request. The village shop is nothing of the sort, rather being a lovely NT tea room with tables in the garden - Tel: 01367 252142.

Kelmscott   Map 46
Morris' opinion that Kelmscott represents 'heaven on earth' is not much wide of the mark. His beloved Manor House is managed by the Society of Antiquaries and flings its doors open to a culture hungry public on Wednesdays and Saturdays from April to October. Tel: 01367 252486 - GL7 3HJ Refreshments are available at such times and a shop deals in Morris memorabilia. The Plough Inn (Tel: 01367 253543 - GL7 3HG) has flagstone floors -

always a reassuring sign - and offers good food and comfortable accommodation. Refurbished 2015.

Radcot   Map 47
The Swan Hotel (Tel: 01367 810220 - OX18 2SX) by Radcot Bridge boasts a gorgeous waterside garden, serves beers largely from the Greene King portfolio, and provides food and accommodation. Customer moorings on the towpath side immediately east of the bridge.

Bampton   Map 47
... in the Bush as it was appended in the past on account of its isolation - as though one might say: 'Bampton in the Sticks'. Famed for morris dancing, Aunt Sally playing and recently (though implausibly, for it is *meant* to be in Yorkshire) as a filming location for *Downton Abbey*, Bampton retains an air of remoteness that's hard to resist. Resist the urge to try!

Eating & Drinking
THE TROUT - Tadpole Bridge. Tel: 01367 870382. Thames-side Trout take two. This one's a gastro

pub/boutique hotel but doesn't disdain to serve thirsty walkers/boaters. SN7 8RF
MORRIS CLOWN - High Street (village centre, a 'country mile' north of Rushey Lock). Tel: 01993 850217. *Good Beer Guide* listed pub run by the same family for two generations. Aunt Sally in the garden and morris dancing at the drop of a hat. OX18 2JW.
BIZTRO - Market Square. Tel: 01993 851151. Stylish little restaurant open Tue-Sat from 6pm. OX18 2JH *Three other pubs, a cafe, and a Chinese take-away.*

Shopping
Co-op convenience store, post office, and an excellent butcher called Patrick Strainge who does home made pies and prize-winning sausages. HSBC bank open Mon & Fri only, 10am-3pm.

Connections
BUSES - Stagecoach services 18 & 19 interleave at Bampton forming links to/from Carterton and Witney, and Eynsham and Oxford. Not Suns.
Tel: 0871 200 2233.
TAXIS - Bampton Cars. Tel: 01993 851900.

47 UPPER THAMES Bampton 5mls/2lks/2hrs

A plethora of drainage dykes and channels serves to emphasise how marshy this district once was, and would be again without mankind's innate inclination to control. Second World War fortifications provide a surreal accompaniment to the river which, like the Kennet & Avon Canal twenty miles to the south, was perceived as a strategic line of defence in the event of invasion. They look foolish now and inadequate, but conflict is always just around the corner, as the war planes flying out of Brize Norton to the north all too frequently and frighteningly confirm. One feels safer with antiquities such as Radcot Bridge, 13th century in origin and generally regarded as the oldest on the Thames, though possibly predated by a Saxon structure. All of which is academic to boaters, who pass beneath an upstart new bridge engineered by William Jessop in 1790 as part of improvements to the Upper Thames carried out in conjunction with the opening of the Thames & Severn Canal. With its humped-back and simple single arch, it has all the hallmarks of a canal bridge, but its location on a double bend, requires concentration.

Radcot Lock features an entertaining canoe pass. In 1954 an American B47 bomber crashed hereabouts in mysterious circumstances during the Cold War. Between Radcot and Rushey locks the river's curves are as pronounced as the beaks of the curlews which call and trill mellifluously overhead. Narrowboat captains have their work cut out to follow the channel. In contrast, the Thames Path isn't averse to cutting corners. Opportunities abound to improvise informal moorings and revel in this most ethereal of landscapes. Rymers and paddles at Rushey Weir were replaced by three radial gates in 2013. Tadpole Bridge was built in 1802 and consists of a single arch. There was a coal wharf here in days gone by.

A4095 to Witney

Bampton

WC

A4095 to Faringdon

Morris Clown

B4449

Highmoor Brook

Rainbow Farm

Meadow Farm

Great Brook

Radcot Cut

weir !

Old Man's Bridge

Radcot Lock
4ft 10ins
Tel: 01367 240676

pb

pb

sharp bends !

Thames Path

Tadpole Bridge

weir !

Rushey Lock
6ft 0ins
Tel: 01367 870218

Trout Inn

Radcot Swan Hotel

Radcot Bridge

46

A4095 to Faringdon

The Thames Path swaps banks at Radcot Bridge and Rushey Lock. A fairly easy to follow footpath leads from Rushey Lock to Bampton; about three-quarters of an hour's walk accompanied by larksong and linseed fields.

pb = WW II pill-box

for details of facilities at Radcot and Bampton turn back to page 91

92

ENGLAND doesn't get much emptier than this. There are more ramblers on Kinder Scout; more boaters on the BCN. Conscientious guide-book compilers hesitate to advocate the Upper Thames' charms, lest they upset its naturally self-effacing equilibrium. But *Canal Companion* devotees are sensitive types who know better than to disturb the *genius loci*; know when to leave well alone.

It becomes increasingly apparent why the Upper Thames bargemen of the 19th century favoured the North Wilts and Wilts & Berks canal route between Cricklade and Abingdon over this narrow and convoluted watercourse. Between the alliterative and contrasting spans of Tadpole and Tenfoot, the river coils its way around a poplar plantation whose denizens are forever shaking their leaves in a susurration of censure: whether at your tillermanship or walking garb it is difficult to say. Red Devons graze Chimney Meadows, a nature reserve of national importance.

Its isolation, its fragile simplicity, suggest that Tenfoot Bridge may have been erected by public-spirited elves. The name has nothing to do with its height, but rather the width of a weir in the vicinity in earlier times. Pound locks came painfully slowly to the Upper Thames.

Shifford Lock - together with a new cut which sliced off an extravagant loop in the river - wasn't opened until the year of Victoria's Diamond Jubilee; a year proudly displayed on the lock-keeper's house which had to wait over a century to receive mains water, sewerage and electricity. The Thames hereabouts used to form the boundary between Oxfordshire to the north and Berkshire to the south. Thanks to Edward Heath it is Oxon. on both banks now. Topic for discussion - is change invariably a dynamic for good, or a chronic human mechanism designed to compensate for inactivity? We oscillate from reorganization to reorganization, yet remain as far as ever from the rainbow's end of perfection. Shifford derives its name from 'sheep ford' and was once a much busier spot than the sequestered farm and Victorian chapel evident today. Alfred the Great held a parliament here in 885. Cromwell pursued The Levellers across the ford at Duxford in 1649. History leaves its calling card at every bend on the Thames.

Shifford

Great Brook

Shifford Lock
7ft 4ins
Tel: 01367
870247

Chimney

Chimney Meadows (nat res)

Weir !

Weir !

pb

S Bends !

Thames Side Farm

nat res

pb

pb = WW II pill-box

Thames Path

Tenfoot Bridge

Duxford

ford

The Thames Path is well sign-posted but can occasionally get overgrown in summer. Best to have some implement with you to ward off the nettles and thistles.

to Longworth (pub)

Harrowdown Hill

325ft

by-road to Hinton Waldrist

Aspects of the Upper Thames

Binsey

Northmoor Rowers

St John's Lock

BUSCOT VILLAGE SHOP

Thames Pathers

G.B. & P.A. HEARNDEN
WORCESTER
EASON MAY
No 4

Buscot

Godstow Trout

S Bends Bampton Way

Boathouse, Appleton

Kelmscott Manor

49 UPPER THAMES Newbridge & Bablock Hythe 5mls/11k/1hr

NEWBRIDGE illustrates the inadvisability of ever labelling anything 'new', for the New Bridge in question is the second oldest on the river, dating from the middle of the 13th century, and being 'new' only in relation to Radcot.

The languorously-named River Windrush has its source near Bourton-on-the-Water up in the Cotswolds, and flows down through Burford and the blanket-making town of Witney. It sidles in to the Thames just upstream of the bridge - blink and you'll miss it. Wilson MacArthur wrote a book about it (published by Cassell as part of a series of river-following books) after the Second World War, when, grateful for having held on to what we might well have lost - as a nation and as individuals - there was still a market for such homespun topographical titles. Now we prefer our vicarious travels to be conducted ideally in more Palinesquely exotic climes.

It would be pleasant to lean over the lichened parapet of one of its upstream facing arches, watch the waters of the Windrush adding their weight to the Thames, and consider the scene here in 1644 when Cromwell's troops captured the bridge from the Royalists following the briefest skirmish, were the Abingdon to Witney road not so busy nowadays.

Hart's Footbridge, marks the site of an old flash weir. A mid 18th century weir-keeper's daughter here was wooed and won by an aristocratic Oxford undergraduate. They married in Northmoor Church in 1766 and lived happily ever after. 'A willowy landscape of meadows and copses' wrote our old canoeing hero William Bliss in 1934: 'England in excelsis'. To our eye there are moments when it is caught impersonating the Nene or the Warwickshire Avon, and we fell just as readily as for these buttercup-runneth-over meadows; spotting an oyster-catcher and a corn bunting in quick succession.

Marked by four tall Lombardy poplars (and a rather less romantic line of electricity pylons), Northmoor Lock dates from those late 19th century improvements to the Upper Thames. This is one of the last Thames' locks to employ paddles and rymers to control the flow of water over the weir.

It can be disorientating to discover the Thames flowing *north* as is the

case in the vicinity of Bablock Hythe. Without the natural obstacle of the Cumnor Hills, it might have missed Oxford entirely (and where, then, would the dark blue boat crew be?) and headed directly for the sea via Abingdon, only half a dozen miles from Bablock Hythe by road, but nearly twenty by water. Ideally you need copies of Matthew Arnold's *The Scholar Gypsy* and *Thyrsis* with you, lengthy mid-19th century poems which echo the mellow, elegiac beauty of the Upper Thames: 'Or in my boat I lie, moor'd to the cool bank in the summer heats, 'mid wide grass meadows which the sunshine fills,' are lines which modern day explorers of the Upper Thames can readily relate to. Laurence (*For the Fallen*) Binyon also wrote a poem entitled *Bab-Lock-Hythe*. There has been a well-known (and loved) ferry here for centuries, but in recent years its operation has been rather erratic. Researching this edition, the vessel itself lay disconsolately on the bank, weighed down by weeds and water*. Its owner, landlord of the somewhat ironically named Ferryman Inn, faces onerous safety cases and insurance stipulations before he can arrange for it to ply again; something, he assured us, he would dearly like to do.

*Though by the time of this reprint it had vanished entirely!

Newbridge
Map 49
Eating & Drinking
THE ROSE REVIVED - riverside (north bank), customer moorings. Tel: 01865 300221. Famous riverbank hostelry operated by Old English Inns, part of the Greene King group. Breakfasts from 7.30am; lunches from 11am; dinners from 5pm. Punt hire - Tel: 07753 276145. OX29 7QD
THE MAYBUSH - riverside (south bank), customer moorings. Tel: 01865 300624. Derelict on the occasion of our most recent survey, but signs of work 2015!
Connections
BUSES - Stagecoach service X15 operates bi-hourly Mon-Sat between Witney and Abingdon, both nice towns to visit. Tel: 0871 200 2233.

Bablock Hythe
Map 49
Up until 1965 the ferry was capable of carrying road vehicles, offering a useful shortcut between Cumnor and Stanton Harcourt. Since then its fortunes have fluctuated, and, in its periodic absences, there have been not unreasonable calls for the provision of a footbridge for the benefit of walkers and cyclists.
Eating & Drinking
THE FERRYMAN INN - riverside. Tel: 01865 880028. Friendly family run free house serving Wadworth beers and guests. Bar/restaurant food, and accommodation. OX29 5AT
Connections
BUSES - Stagecoach service No.18 offers Mon-Sat links with Oxford and Bampton, rendering Bablock Hythe a useful staging post for Thames Path walkers. Tel: 0871 200 2233.

Stanton Harcourt
Map 50
Demure Oxfordshire village of thatch and mellow stone whose tri-towered roofline beckons strays in off the riverbank. Alexander Pope stayed here circa 1718 and wrote a poetic epitaph to two young lovers struck dead by lightning. It appears on a stone on the wall of the church which contains fine monuments.
Eating & Drinking
HARCOURT ARMS - Main Road. Tel: 01865 881931. Country pub which doubles as a village shop and post office. Closed for renovation 2015. OX29 5RJ
Connections
BUSES - as Bablock Hythe.

Eynsham
Map 50
A pilgrimage in homage to Temple Thurston's eponymous boatman, Harry, is all but obligatory. And, in any case, the market square, overlooked by St Leonard's church, and a quaint building called the Bartholomew Room, is very pretty.
Eating & Drinking
TALBOT INN - Oxford Road. Tel: 01865 881348 . Arkells pub offering both food and accommodation. Lunch from noon, dinner from 6pm. OX29 4BT
QUEENS HEAD - Queen Street. Tel: 01865 881229. Welcoming town centre pub offering food daily at lunchtimes and on weekday evenings. OX29 4HH
THE BAYLEAF - Lombard Street. Tel: 01865 884401. Indian restaurant. OX29 4HT
EYNSHAM EMPORIUM - Mill Street. Tel: 01865 731717. Coffees, light lunches and teas in stylish cookware and gift shop. OX29 4JS
Shopping
A cluster of independent shops including the Natural Bread Co., Golsby Butchers, The Market Garden (greengrocers and wholefoods), Eynsham Cellars, and Evenlode DIY. Co-op & PO with ATM. Country market on Thursday mornings in the Church Hall.
Connections
BUSES - Stagecoach Gold service S1 runs quarter-hourly (20mins Suns) into the centre of Oxford. Service 18 operates hourly Mon-Sat via Stanton Harcourt to Bampton. Tel: 0871 200 2233.

LOW-BANKED, and at its most northerly, the Thames arcs around the Victorian poet Matthew Arnold's 'green-muffled' Cumnor Hills. Deciduously wooded, and roamed by deer, Wytham (pronounced 'white-ham') Hill marks the highest point of the Cumnor 'range'. Unable to rely on the ferry at Bablock Hythe (Map 49), the Thames Path detours away from the riverbank, rejoining it near Skinner's 'Island' where, up until the 19th century, there was a weir, a mill and an inn. River water is pumped into Farmoor Reservoir which was constructed by the simple expedient of digging a large hole in the ground and lining it with the resultant spoil. A good proportion of its contents finds its way to the bathroom suites of Swindon. Fishing, watersports and bird-watching are amongst the leisure activities additionally engendered by the reservoir. Swinford Toll Bridge was built in 1769 and many consider it one of the most handsome on the Thames. A classically-styled toll house abuts its northern approach, but the keeper spends most of his time in a plastic shelter now, attempting to cope with an estimated four million toll-paying vehicles per annum, traffic volumes that the 18th century Earl of Abingdon can scarcely have envisaged when he bought out the ferry and commissioned the bridge.

Vying with the Windrush when it comes to lovely river names, the Evenlode makes its entry a little over a mile downstream of Eynsham Lock. The river's source lies near Stow-on-the-Wold and it flows down through the remnants of the ancient Forest of Wychwood. It was too shallow and meandering a river ever to be practically navigable, but at the beginning of the 19th century, the Duke of Marlborough funded the construction of Cassington Cut, a canal not quite a mile long, mainly to serve the mill at Cassington but also as an outlet for Eynsham malt. Cassington was a 'halt' on the Oxford to Fairford railway. Predominantly hauled by 'Pannier' tank locomotives, the last passenger train trundled off stage forever in 1962. Paul Jennings wrote wistfully about its demise in *Just A Few Lines*, long out of print but reasonably easily obtained secondhand.

Stanton Harcourt

Eynsham (csd : 1962)
WC
P
Town Centre
Eynsham

Thames Path

Pinkhill Lock
3ft 6ins
Tel: 01865 881452

Skinner's Island

Weir !

Oxford Cruisers
Anglo-Welsh

B4449

Talbot Inn

Swinford Toll Bridge
weir !

B4044

Eynsham Lock
2ft 9ins
Tel: 01865 881324

Thames Path

Cassington Cut

R. Evenlode

A40

Cassington (csd - 1962)

Farmoor Reservoir

Farmoor

Wytham Hill 539 ft

Wytham Great Wood

for details of facilities at Stanton Harcourt and Eynsham turn back to page 97

This Guide

Pearson's Canal Companions are a long established, independently produced series of guide books devoted to the inland waterways, and designed to appeal equally to boaters, walkers, cyclists and other, less readily pigeon-holed members of society. Considerable pride is taken to make these guides as up to date, accurate, entertaining and inspirational as possible. A good guide book should fulfil three functions: make you want to go; interpret the lie of the land when you're there; and provide a lasting souvenir of your journeys. It is to be hoped that this guide ticks all three boxes, and possibly more besides.

The Maps

There are fifty-four numbered maps whose layout is shown by the Route Planner inside the front cover. Maps 1 to 16 cover the Oxford Canal between Hawkesbury, on the outskirts of Coventry, and Oxford where there is a link to the Thames.

Maps 17 to 39 cover the Grand Union Canal between Braunston and Brentford/Paddington. Maps 19A, 28A, 28B and 35A cover the Northampton, Aylesbury, Wendover and Slough arms respectively.

Maps 40 to 44 cover the Leicester Section of the Grand Union Canal between Norton Junction (near Daventry) and Market Harborough.

Maps 45 to 50 cover the Upper Thames from Lechlade to Oxford.

The maps - measured imperially like the waterways they depict, and not being slavishly north-facing - are easily read in either direction. Users will thus find most itineraries progressing smoothly and logically from left to right or vice versa. Figures quoted at the top of each map refer to distance per map, locks per map and average cruising time.

INFORMATION

An alternative indication of timings from centre to centre can be found on the Route Planner. Obviously, cruising times vary with the nature of your boat and the number of crew at your disposal, so quoted times should be taken only as an estimate. Neither do times quoted take into account any delays which might occur at lock flights in high season. Walking and cycling times will depend very much on the state of individual sections of towpath and stamina.

The Text

Each map is accompanied by a route commentary placing the waterway in its historic, social and topographical context. As close to each map as is feasible, gazetteer-like entries are given for places passed through, listing, where appropriate, facilities of significance to users of this guide. Every effort is made to ensure these details are as up to date as possible, but - especially where pubs/restaurants are concerned - we suggest you telephone ahead if relying upon an entry to provide you with a meal at any given time.

Walking

The simplest way to explore the inland waterways is on foot along towpaths originally provided so that horses could 'tow' boats. Walking costs little more than the price of shoe leather and you are free to concentrate on the passing scene; something that boaters, with the responsibilities of navigation thrust upon them, are not always at liberty to do. The maps set out to give some idea of the quality of the towpath on any given section of canal. More of an art than a science to be sure, but at least it reflects our personal experiences, and whilst it does vary from area to area, none of it should prove problematical for anyone inured to the vicissitudes of country walking. The Upper Thames is accompanied by the Thames Path, well sign-posted and usually pretty good underfoot.

We recommend the use of public transport to facilitate 'one-way' itineraries but stress the advisability of checking up-to-date details on the telephone numbers quoted, or on the websites of National Rail Enquiries or Traveline for trains and buses respectively. As reliable as we trust this guide will be, the additional use of a contemporary Ordnance Survey Landranger or Explorer sheet is recommended as they are
continued overleaf:

continued from page 99:

able to present your chosen route in a broader context. Should you be considering walking the full length of these paths over several consecutive days, the dwindling band of Tourist Information Centres can usually be relied upon to offer accommodation advice.

Cycling

Bicycling along towpaths is an increasingly popular pastime, though one not always equally popular with other waterway users such as boaters, anglers and pedestrians. It is important to remember that you are sharing the towpath with other people out for their own form of enjoyment, and to treat them with the respect and politeness they deserve. A bell is a useful form of diplomacy; failing that, a stentorian cough or the ability to whistle tunefully; light operatic extracts go down very well in our experience. Happily, since the inception of the Canal & River Trust, it is no longer necessary for cyclists to acquire a permit to use the towpath. The Thames Path is not designated for cycling between Lechlade and Oxford.

Boating

Boating on inland waterways is an established, though relatively small, facet of the UK tourist industry. It is also, increasingly, a chosen lifestyle. There are approximately 30,000 privately owned boats registered on the inland waterways, but in addition to these, a number of firms offer boats for hire. These range from small operators with half a dozen boats to sizeable fleets run by companies with several bases.

Most hire craft have all the creature comforts you are likely to expect. In the excitement of planning a boating holiday you may give scant thought to the contents of your hire boat, but at the end of a hard day's boating such matters take on more significance, and a well equipped, comfortable boat, large enough to accommodate your crew with something to spare, can make the difference between a good holiday and one which will be shudderingly remembered for the wrong reasons. Traditionally, hire boats are booked by the week or fortnight, though many firms now offer more flexible short breaks or extended weeks. All reputable hire firms give newcomers tuition in boat handling and lock working, and first-timers soon find themselves adapting to the pace of things 'on the cut'.

Navigational Advice

Newcomers, hiring a boat on the inland waterways for the first time, have every right to expect sympathetic and thorough tuition from the company providing their boat. Boat-owners are, by definition, likely to be already adept at navigating; though not necessarily with the more demanding locks of the Grand Union, or a river such as the Thames. So here are some helpful hints in advance of experience.

Locks are part of the charm of inland waterway cruising, but they can be potentially dangerous environments for children, pets and careless adults. Use of them should be methodical and unhurried, whilst special care should be exercised in rain, frost and snow when slippery hazards abound.

In urban areas CART often attach security appliances to the paddle gear to prevent spurious use of the locks by hooligans. Boaters should ensure that they have at least one - but preferably two or three - 'handcuff' and/or CART facilities keys with which to gain access to the locks thus treated.

Locks on the routes covered in this guide come in various shapes and sizes. On the Oxford Canal they are narrow and present few difficulties in operation. On the Grand Union Canal they are wide and rather heavier to operate. Their greater width, however, enables two narrow boats to share the lock, and locks shared means worked shared, a bonus in most cases.

The locks on that part of the Leicester Section of the Grand Union included in this guide are narrow, and largely grouped in 'staircase' flights at Watford and Foxton where lock-keepers will usually be on hand to help and advise.

On the Upper Thames the locks are wide and, with the exception of Godstow, hand-operated. Traditionally they have always been manned (usually by avuncular bastions of river lore) and continue to be so in high season. But, increasingly, off-peak and at quiet times 'self-service' applies, which is fine by most boaters, because the locks are a treat to work, and copious operating procedures are prominently displayed. As on the canals, be methodical. The major difference being that the sluice gear is operated by wheels as opposed to windlasses. And actually, it's rather fun: astride the lockgate, spinning the wheel, you can imagine yourself steering a keel up the Stainforth & Keadby. A *Cruising Guide to the River Thames* is available from the Environment Agency.

Finally, it behoves us all to be on our best behaviour at locks. Remember to exercise a little 'give and take'. The use of foul mouths or fists to decide precedence at locks is one canal tradition not worthy of preservation.

Moveable Bridges are an occasional feature of the routes included in this guide. Some 'swing', some 'lift', some are manually or windlass-operated, some mechanised. Most require either a CART facilities key and/or 'handcuff' key to facilitate their moving. Always return them to the position you found them in after use unless it is obvious that another boat is approaching to use them.

Tunnels occur at a number of points on the Oxford and Grand Union canals and a great fun to negotiate. Pets and young children should be kept 'indoors'. Passages of broad beam boats through Braunston and Blisworth tunnels is severely restricted and must be pre-booked with the Canal & River Trust.

Mooring on the canals featured in this guide is per usual practice - ie on the towpath side, away from sharp bends, bridge-holes and narrows. Theoretically, you can moor anywhere - as long as the foregoing stipulations are taken into account - but in recent years navigation authorities have signposted designated visitor mooring sights, often with time limitations to dissuade lingering. An open, yellow-tinted bollard symbol on the maps represents such sites; though occasionally we also include this symbol if we feel the location especially lends itself to short term mooring but isn't officially designated. Mooring on the Upper Thames can be more problematical. There is little formal provision, but every opportunity to improvise informally, often to especially amenable effect.

Turning points on the canals are known as 'winding holes'; pronounced as the thing which blows because in the old days the wind was expected to do much of the work rather than the boatman. Winding holes capable of taking a full length boat of around seventy foot length are marked where appropriate on the maps. Winding holes capable of turning shorter craft are marked with the approximate length. It is of course possible to turn boats at junctions and at most boatyards, though in the case of the latter it is considered polite to seek permission to do so.

Boating facilities are provided at fairly regular intervals along the inland waterways, and range from a simple water tap or refuse disposal skip, to the provision of sewage disposal, showers and laundry. Such vital features are also obtainable at boatyards and marinas along with repairs and servicing.

Closures (or 'stoppages' in canal parlance) traditionally occur on the inland waterways between November and April, during which time most of the heavy maintenance work is undertaken. Occasionally, however, an emergency stoppage, or perhaps water restriction, may be imposed at short notice, closing part of the route you intend to use.

Waterway Authorities
Canal & River Trust
The Canal & River Trust controls the bulk of the inland waterways network. Their Head Office is located at:
First Floor North
Station House
500 Elder Gate
Milton Keynes
MK9 1BB
Tel: 0303 040 4040
www.canalrivertrust.org.uk
Environment Agency
The Environment Agency is responsible for navigation on the River Thames. Their head office is located at:
Kings Meadow House
Kings Meadow Road
Reading
RG1 8DQ
Tel: 03708 506506
www.environment-agency.gov.uk
The EA are also responsible for navigation on the River Nene. If you are proceeding onto that river from the Northampton Arm (Map 19A) you can obtain information from their Kettering office at:
Nene House
Pythchley Lodge Road
Kettering
Northants
NN15 6JN
Tel: 08708 506 506

Societies
The Inland Waterways Association was founded in 1946 to campaign for the retention of the canal system. Many routes now open to pleasure boaters may not have been so but for this organisation. Membership details, together with details of the IWA's regional branches, may be obtained from: Inland Waterways Association, Island House, Moor Road, Chesham HP5 1WA. Tel: 01494 783453.
Aylesbury Canal Society
Bedford & Milton Keynes Waterway Trust
Buckingham Canal Society
Cotswold Canals Trust
Foxton Inclined Plane Trust
Leighton Buzzard Canal Society
Old Union Canal Society
River Thames Society
Wendover Arm Trust
Current membership details of the above groups can be found via the internet or through the Inland Waterways Association.

Acknowledgements
A hand-picked, tight-knit team of specialist contributors combine to create the Canal Companions. Alphabetically they are: Meg Gregory, Hawksworth of Uttoxeter, and Karen Tanguy - huge thanks to them all! Additional thanks to Brian Collings, David Dare, Tom Lumsden, Lynda Payton, and the admirable captain of nb *Lacewing*.

Hire Bases

ABC BOAT HIRE - Rugby, Oxford Canal, Map 4; Gayton Marina, Northampton Arm, Map 19A; Market Harborough, Grand Union Canal, Map 44. PO Box 232, Worcester WR1 2SD Tel: 0330 333 0590. *www.abcboathire.com*

ANGLO WELSH WATERWAY HOLIDAYS - North Kilworth, GU Leicester Section, Map 42; Eynsham, Upper Thames, Map 50. 2 Hide Market, West Street, St Philips, Bristol BS2 0BH Tel: 0117 304 1122. *www.anglowelsh.co.uk*

ARMADA BOAT HIRE - Harborough Magna, Oxford Canal, Map 3. Cathiron Lane, Harborough Magna, Rugby CV23 0HA Tel: 0788 066 0660. *www.armadaboathire.co.uk*

BLACK PRINCE HOLIDAYS - Clifton, Oxford Canal, Map 4; Napton, Oxford Canal, Map 7; Willowtree Marina, Paddington Arm, Map 36. The Wharf, Stoke Prior, Bromsgrove B60 4LA Tel: 01527 575115. *www.black-prince.com*

CALCUTT BOATS - Southam, Grand Union Canal, Map 7. Tomlow Road, Stockton, Southam, Warks CV47 8HX Tel: 01926 813757. *www.calcuttboats.com*

CANAL BOAT CLUB - Gayton Junction, GU Northampton Arm, Map 19A; Market Harborough, GU Leicester Section, Map 44. PO Box 57 Budleigh Salterton, Devon EX9 7ZN Tel: 01395 443363. *www.canalboatclub.com*

CANAL BREAKS - Hillmorton, Oxford Canal, Map 4. Hillmorton, Rugby, Warks CV21 4PP Tel: 01788 578661. *www.canalbreaks.com*

CLIFTON CRUISERS - Clifton Wharf, Oxford Canal, Map 4. Vicarage Hill, Clifton upon Dunsmore, Rugby, Warks CV23 0DG Tel: 01788 543570. *www.cliftoncruisers.com*

BOATING DIRECTORY

COLLEGE CRUISERS - Oxford, Oxford Canal, Map 16. Combe Road, Oxford OX2 6BL Tel: 01865 554343. *www.collegecruisers.com*

COTSWOLD BOAT HIRE - Lechlade, Upper Thames, Map 45. Trout Inn, Lechlade, Glos. GL7 3HA Tel: 01793 727083. *www.cotswoldboat.co.uk*

LIME FARM MARINA - Cathiron, Oxford Canal, Map 3. Cathiron, Rugby, Warks CV23 0JH Tel: 01788 570131. *www.limefarmmarina.co.uk*

NORTH KILWORTH WHARF - North Kilworth, Leicester Section, Map 42. Station Road, North Kilworth, Lutterworth, Leics LE17 6JB Tel: 01858 881723. *www.northkilworthwharf.com*

NAPTON NARROWBOATS - Napton, Oxford Canal, Map 7. Napton Marina, Stockton, Southam, Warks CV47 8HX Tel: 01926 813644. *www.napton-marina.co.uk*

OXFORDSHIRE NARROWBOATS - Lower Heyford, Oxford Canal, Map 13. Heyford Wharf, Station Road, Lower Heyford, Oxfordshire. OX25 5PD Tel: 01869 340348. *www.oxfordshire-narrowboats.co.uk*

PUDDLING CRUISERS - Milton Keynes Marina, Grand Union Canal, Map 13. MK6 3BX Lilac Cottage, Colchester Road, Chappel. CO6 2AA Tel: 020 8123 3612. *www.puddlingcruisers.co.uk*

ROSE NARROWBOATS - Stretton-under-Fosse, Oxford Canal, Map 2. Fosse Way, Stretton-under-Fosse, Rugby, Warks. CV23 0PU Tel: 01788 832449. *www.rose-narrowboats.co.uk*

SAISONS - Hillmorton, Oxford Canal, Map 5. Canal Shop, Hillmorton Wharf, Crick Road, Rugby, Warks CV21 4PW Tel: 01327 844442. *www.saisons.co.uk*

TWYFORD WHARF - Adderbury, Oxford Canal, Map 11. Old Barn, Twyford Wharf, Adderbury, Banbury OX17 3JN Tel: 01295 816025 *www.narrowboatholidays.com*

UNION CANAL CARRIERS - Braunston, Grand Union Canal, Map 6. Bottom Lock, Braunston, Northants. NN11 7HJ Tel: 01788 890784. *www.unioncanalcarriers.co.uk*

WILLOW WREN - Rugby, Oxford Canal, Map 4. Rugby Wharf, Consul Road, Rugby, Warks. CV21 1PB Tel: 01788 562183. *www.willowwren.co.uk*

WYVERN SHIPPING - Linslade, Grand Union Canal, Map 26. Rothschild Road, Linslade, Leighton Buzzard, Beds LU7 2TF Tel: 01525 372355. *www.canalholidays.co.uk*

Day Boat Hire

COSGROVE NARROWBOAT Co. - Cosgrove, Grand Union, Map 22. Tel: 01525 372853. MK19 7JR

DENHAM DAY BOATS - Denham, Grand Union Canal, Map 34. Tel: 01895 271070. UB9 4AF

FOXTON BOAT SERVICES - Foxton, Leicester Section, Map 44. Tel: 0116 279 2285. LE16 7RA

UNION WHARF - Market Harborough, Leicester Section, Map 44. Tel: 01858 432123. LE16 7UW

Boatyards

APSLEY MARINA - Apsley, Grand Union Canal, Map 31. Tel: 01895 449851. HP3 9FP

BATES BOATYARD - Aylesbury Arm, Map 28A. Tel: 01296 632017. HP23 4PS

BAXTER BOATFITTING - Yardley Gobion, Grand Union, Map 21. Tel: 01908 542844. NN12 7UE

BLISWORTH MARINA - Blisworth, Grand Union, Map 19. Tel: 01604 879827. NN7 3FG

BLISWORTH TUNNEL - Blisworth, Grand Union, Map 20. Tel: 01604 858868. NN7 3BN

BRAUNSTON BOATS - Braunston, Grand Union, Map 6. Tel: 01788 891079. NN11 7HJ

BRAUNSTON MARINA - Braunston, Grand Union, Map 6. Tel: 01788 891373. NN11 7JH

BRIDGEWATER BOATS - Watford, Grand Union Canal, Map 32. Tel: 01923 211448. WD18 8SN

BRINKLOW BOAT SERVICES - Stretton Stop, Oxford Canal, Map 2. Tel: 01788 833331. CV23 0PR

BULBOURNE DRYDOCK - Bulbourne, Grand Union Canal, Map 28. See Bates Boatyard.

CALCUTT BOATS - Southam, Grand Union Canal, Map 7. Tel: 01926 813757. CV47 8HX

CLIFTON CRUISERS - Clifton Wharf, Oxford Canal, Map 4. Tel: 01788 543570. CV23 0EY

COLLEGE CRUISERS - Combe Road, Oxford, Map 16. Tel: 01865 554343. OX2 6BL

COWROAST MARINA - Cowroast, Grand Union Canal, Map 29. Tel: 01442 823222. HP23 5RE

CRICK MARINA - Crick, Leicester Section, Map 41. Tel: 01788 824034. NN6 7SQ

CROPREDY MARINA - Cropredy, Oxford Canal, Map 9. Tel: 01295 758911. OX17 1JP

DENHAM MARINA - Uxbridge, Grand Union Canal, Map 34. Tel: 01895 239811. UB8 1NB

FENNY MARINA - Fenny Compton, Oxford Canal, Map 8. Tel: 01295 770461. CV47 2XD

FOXTON BOAT SERVICES - Foxton, Leicester Section, Map 44. Tel: 0116 279 2285. LE16 7RA

GAYTON MARINA - Gayton, GU Northampton Arm, Maps 19/19A. Tel: 01604 858685. NN7 3ER

GRAND JUNCTION BOAT CO - Gayton Junction, GUC, Map 19. Tel: 01604 858043.

GROVE LOCK MARINA - Grove Lock, Grand Union, Map 26. Tel: 01525 377444. LU7 0QU

HAREFIELD MARINA - Harefield, Grand Union Canal, Map 33. Tel: 01895 822036. UB9 6PD

HEYFORD FIELDS MARINA - Bugbrooke, Grand Union, Map 19. Tel: 01604 833599. NN7 3NP

HIGH LINE YACHTING - Cowley Peachey, Grand Union Canal, Map 35, UB8 2JS; Iver, Slough Arm, Map 35A, SL0 9RG. Northolt, Paddington Arm, Map 38. UB5 6AG Tel: 01753 651496.

HILLMORTON WHARF - Hillmorton, Oxford Canal, Map 4. Tel: 01788 540149. CV21 4PW

KINGFISHER MARINA - Yardley Gobion, Grand Union Canal, Map 21. Tel: 01908 542293. NN12 7UE

LIME FARM MARINA - Cathiron, Oxford Canal, Map 3. Tel: 01788 570131. CV23 0JH

MIDDX & HERTS BOAT SERVICES - Winkwell, GU, Map 30. Tel: 01442 872985. HP1 2RZ

MILTON KEYNES MARINA - Milton Keynes, Grand Union, Map 23. Tel: 01908 672672. MK6 3BX

NAPTON NARROWBOATS - Napton, Oxford Canal, Map 7. Tel: 01926 813644. CV47 8HX

NORTHAMPTON MARINA - Northampton, River Nene, Map 19A. Tel: 01604 604344. NN1 5NL

NORTH KILWORTH WHARF - Kilworth, L'ster Section, Map 42. Tel: 01858 881723. LE17 6JB

OXFORD CRUISERS - Eynsham, River Thames, Map 50. Tel: 01865 881698. OX29 4DA

OXFORDSHIRE NARROWBOATS - Heyford, Oxford Canal, Map 13. Tel: 01869 340348. OX25 5PD

PACKET BOAT MARINA - Cowley Peachey, Grand Union, Map 35. Tel: 01895 449851. UB8 2JJ

P&S MARINE - Watford, Grand Union Canal, Map 32. Tel: 01923 248372. WD18 8SN

ROSE NARROWBOATS - Stretton-under-Fosse, Oxford Canal, Map 2. Tel: 01788 832449. CV23 0PU

RUGBY BOAT SALES - Weedon, Grand Union Canal, Map 18. Tel: 01327 342211. NN7 4SF

SOVEREIGN WHARF - Banbury, Oxford Canal, Map 10. Tel: 01295 275657. OX16 2PP

THRUPP WHARF MARINA - Cosgrove, Grand Union Canal, Map 22. Tel: 01908 542113. MK19 7BE

TOOLEY'S BOATYARD - Banbury, Oxford Canal, Map 10. Tel: 01295 272917. OX16 2PQ

UNION CANAL CARRIERS - Braunston, Grand Union, Map 6. Tel: 01788 890784. NN11 7HJ

UNION WHARF - Market Harborough, Leicester Section, Map 44. Tel: 01858 432123. LE16 7AU

UXBRIDGE BOAT CENTRE - Uxbridge, Grand Union Canal, Map 34. Tel: 01895 252019. UX8 2QX

WALKER SERVICES - Aynho Wharf, Oxford Canal, Map 12. Tel: 01869 338483. OX17 3PB

WELFORD MARINA - Welford, Leicester Section, Map 42. Tel: 01858 575995. NN6 7JQ

WELTONFIELD NARROWBOATS - Welton, L'ster Section, Map 17. Tel: 01327 842282. NN11 2LG

WHILTON MARINA - Whilton, Northants, Grand Union Canal, Map 17. Tel: 01327 842577. NN11 2NH

WILLOWBRIDGE MARINA - Stoke Hammond, Grand Union, Map 24. Tel: 01908 643242. MK2 3JZ

WILLOWTREE MARINA - Paddington Arm, Map 36. Tel: 0208 841 6585. UB4 9TB

WILLOW WREN - Rugby, Oxford Canal, Map 4. Tel: 01788 562183. CV21 1PB

WYVERN SHIPPING - Linslade, Grand Union Canal, Map 26. Tel: 01525 372355. LU7 2TF

YELVERTOFT MARINA - Yelvertoft, Leicester Section, Map 41. Tel: 01788 822292. NN6 6AL

Nine More Reasons for Exploring the Canals with Pearsons

9th edition - ISBN 978 0 9562777 3 2

10th edition - ISBN 978 0 9562777 8 7

9th edition - ISBN 978 0 9562777 7 0

1st edition - ISBN 978 0 9928492 1 4

7th edition - ISBN 978 0 9562777 5 6

8th edition - ISBN 978 0 9562777 2 5

9th edition - ISBN 978 0 9562777 4 9

1st edition - ISBN 978 0 9928492 0 7

3rd edition - ISBN 978 0 9562777 6 3

Pearson's Canal Companions are published by Wayzgoose. They are widely available from hire bases, boatyards, canal shops, good bookshops, via Amazon and other internet outlets.